Library of
Davidson College

IN HOC SIGNO?

KENNIKAT PRESS

NATIONAL UNIVERSITY PUBLICATIONS

SERIES IN AMERICAN STUDIES

Under the General Editorial Supervision of

JAMES P. SHENTON

Professor of History, Columbia University

GLEN GABERT

IN HOC SIGNO?

*A Brief History of
Catholic Parochial Education
in America*

National University Publications
KENNIKAT PRESS
Port Washington, N.Y./ London

Copyright © 1973 by Glen Gabert. All Rights Reserved. No part of this publication may be reproduced, stored in a retrieval system, or transmitted, in any form or by any means, electronic, mechanical, photocopying, recording, or otherwise, without the prior written permission of the publisher.

Library of Congress Catalog Card No.: 72-89992
ISBN: 0-8046-9028-6

Manufactured in the United States of America

Published by
Kennikat Press, Inc.
Port Washington, N.Y./London

*To my brother,
Gregory*

Foreword

The Roman Catholic parochial school system in the United States of America is unique in the history of western education. It is the largest private school system in the United States. It is the largest private elementary school system in the world and in the history of the world. Unlike most other private school systems, it does not draw its enrollment from an elite social class, but rather it is within the financial grasp of the masses. Technically speaking, a parochial school is a private and denominational school that is supported by a single church unit or parish. These individual parish schools are drawn together into a series of diocesan systems throughout the country.

Though few foresaw it a decade ago, the Roman Catholic school system has entered into a period of unprecedented decline. Between 1965 and 1971 enrollments fell by at least 900,000 and the actual number of school units dropped by about one thousand. The future of these schools is of grave concern to all Americans, Roman Catholics, and non-Roman Catholics. For many years Catholic schools provided an education for a significant segment of the population at a tremendous savings to the American taxpayer. They have been of inestimable value to the public schools if for no other reason than they helped to keep them more accountable to the general public by offering a viable educational alternative.

This book is an attempt to present a history of this remarkable educational phenomenon—the parochial schools. The point of reference adopted in this book has been that of official documents, but not merely a summary or commentary of these writings but rather a presentation of them in historical context. Papal writings, official pronouncements, and statements of the American hierarchy form the major corpus of these documents. A careful reading of these writings suggests several questions for which attempted answers have been given in this book: Have the official writings of the Church had any really significant effect on the course of the history of American Catholic parochial education? Have these documents revealed any special insight or understanding of the issues at stake on the part of the persons issuing them? What influence have the papal documents had upon the schools? What of the statements of the American hierarchy, have they been markedly influenced by papal pronouncements and *vice versa?* Based on the significance and effectiveness of past pronouncements, what might be expected of contemporary and future pronouncements?

There is much contemporary debate about the parochial schools. Some feel that they should be preserved unchanged; others feel that they should be radically altered; still others feel that they should be abandoned. Yet, what is so surprising, very few persons seem to know anything of the real history of these schools; they see the red brick building next to the church but never stop to ask how it came to be there or why it was built. Church history for too many persons still consists of tracing the travels of Saint Paul on a map. Unfortunately, though most Americans have attended some sort of school, they have little knowledge about the history of education. Have the Catholic schools been a success or a failure? To answer this one must determine what they were intended to do. Despite all their shortcomings, Catholic schools have made a tremendous positive contribution to the American culture.

The first Catholic educational institutions in America were staffed by Spanish and French clergy, generations before the settlement of Jamestown in 1607. Though some historians have interpreted the origins of Catholicity in the United States to be in these early stirrings, the Roman Catholic Church found its real roots in the United States in Maryland and other southern settlements of seventeenth-century English Catholics. The Catholic school system does not date from this period, however, nor does it go back to the Irish activities during the first half of the nineteenth century. The Irish gave the Church its muscle power, its aggressive self-confidence. Contemporaneous with the common school movement, these Irish often supported the erection of parish schools. Attendance in them was not usually considered mandatory. It was not the Irish who arranged them into diocesan systems. Rather it was the Germans coming to America after the Civil War who were the real founders of the Roman Catholic parochial school system in the United States. Distrustful of a culture markedly different from their own, drawn together by a common language that was not understood in the new country, comparatively better off than their Irish immigrant predecessors, accustomed to supporting Church schools with some public assistance in the Old Country, the Germans were disposed to supporting parish schools as an alternative to public education.

In the latter nineteenth century, the older, more Americanized immigrant groups such as the Irish were not so eager as the Germans to support separate private schools. Only a complicated series of diplomatic maneuvers gained papal support for the German position. The Vatican, perhaps conditioned by a sad series of experiences beginning with Napoleon and his imprisonment of Pius VII and extending over the next century and a quarter to the Fascist era of Mussolini, was disposed to see things the way the Germans did. Most American Catholics came to pay at least lip service to the concept of parochial education. Few questioned the ideal of every Catholic child in a Catholic school until recent years. The present times are marked by a Catholic school crisis — not the first in American history. It is really not possible to plan adequately for the future unless one can realistically assess the present. A knowledge of the recent past makes any such assessment easier. This study is not intended as a blueprint for future policy but rather as an analysis of the official policies that have directed the schools to the present day.

The author would like to acknowledge with gratitude the special assistance of Gerald Gutek, John Wozniak, and Rosemary Donatelli, all of Loyola University of Chicago, in the preparation of the manuscript. He would also like to thank Mary Quinn and Irene Gabert for the hours they spent typing and proofreading. The research for this book was made possible by a grant secured through the office of Dean Raymond Mariella at Loyola from the Arthur J. Schmitt Foundation.

Finally, the author would like to point out that, although he did not always preface the word "Catholic" with the adjective "Roman" throughout the text, he was not implying by this omission that "Catholicism" and "Roman Catholicism" are exact synonyms.

Contents

FOREWORD		vii
I	THE ERA OF THE ENGLISH: *From Discovery to 1829*	3
II	THE ERA OF THE IRISH: *1829–1866*	20
III	THE ERA OF THE GERMANS: *1866–1919*	44
IV	THE GOLDEN ERA: *1919–1958*	80
V	THE ERA OF THE AMERICANS: *1958– – – –*	99
VI	EPILOGUE	119

APPENDIX

    CHRONOLOGICAL SUMMARY — 126
    CATHOLIC SCHOOL SYSTEM IN 1900 — 128
    CATHOLIC SCHOOLS IN AMERICA BY YEARS — 129

SUGGESTIONS FOR FURTHER READING — 133

INDEX — 137

IN HOC SIGNO?

I
The Era Of The English
FROM DISCOVERY TO 1829

The story of Catholics in America is as old as Columbus; and, if one accepts the Brendan legends or considers the Norsemen the real discoverers, it is even older. Since at least the fourth century, Christian schools and Roman Christianity have gone hand in hand. It is not surprising, therefore, that Catholics in America went about establishing schools very early; but there is disagreement among scholars as to which national group founded the first school in the United States. Claimants for the honor include the Spanish, French, and English. Perhaps a fourth category, German, should be added, but German Catholics of the colonial era lived in an area where the Church was dominated by English adherents.

The Spanish Catholics who settled in Florida and the old Southwest had established schools several decades before the founding of Jamestown, the first permanent English settlement, in 1607. These early Spanish educational enterprises were almost exclusively the work of missionary priests. There was probably a school in New Mexico by 1516 and one in Florida by 1565 or 1594. The Franciscans were operating missions in California by 1629. After 1689 there were Catholic schools in Texas. The earliest secondary school may have been the seminary established at Saint Augustine in 1606. Its curriculum seems to have been a classical one—very typical for Catholic schools until well into the twentieth century. Spanish schools in the old Southwest were staffed and directed through Mexican headquarters, those in Florida, through Cuban offices. The principal Spanish religious community in that area which is now the United

States was the Franciscans.[1] These early Spanish schools were small and, more often than not, centered around a mission. It is almost impossible to discuss enrollment figures with great accuracy or even to fix the exact number of these schools. There were probably no more than several dozen in all. The padre dominated the mission school; he was, one might say, superintendent, principal, teacher, school board, and chaplain. Mission schools were boarding schools. The curriculum was rudimentary: reading, writing, basic arithmetic; trades; and, of course, Christian doctrine. Girls received something of a convent education. The primary aim appears to have been more religious than intellectual. Schools operated for Spanish children, like those in Saint Augustine, followed a somewhat different pattern and were less vocational in orientation and more like a Latin school.

Spain's educational record in the New World, judged by the standards of the time, was a good one. The mission system was, perhaps, the most successful institution developed to deal constructively with the Indian population. The red man faired better here than in British America. Spain was one of the most Roman Catholic countries of Europe. The Church was a vital force in the society, inextricably interwoven into the fabric of Spanish life. The State had a tremendous control over the affairs of the Church, and so Spanish missionaries were really agents of the State as well as religious leaders. The Government supported the mission and paid the friar's salary. It is extremely difficult to see many roots of the contemporary American Catholic school system in these early Spanish undertakings. They bear more resemblance to a kibbutz than a parochial school. Catholicism in the United States does not bear the Spanish stamp. Missionaries in the old Southwest had been driven from the missions by Mexican authorities before the area was incorporated into the American diocesan structure. There is no continuous line between these activities and the present system. They remain, therefore, an interesting and laudable, but largely unconnected, chapter in the history of Catholic education in the United States.

The French Catholics, too, set about founding schools. What was probably the first girls' school in the present-day United States was located in New Orleans in 1727 and staffed by Ursuline nuns. These ladies may well have been the first professional elementary teachers in the country. Bienville, the founder and Governor of New

Orleans, had obtained the services of Capuchins who took over a parish and set up a school for boys, but he had been unsuccessful in persuading the Jesuits to establish a college in Louisiana. These French stirrings, while praiseworthy, were miniscule; the population of New Orleans was only three hundred persons in 1722.

The French influence, of course, was felt outside of Louisiana. There was a French Catholic school in Saint Louis by 1764 and similar schools in Detroit, Vincennes, Kaskaskia, and Makinaw Straits. Jesuits, Recollets, and Capuchins were all laborers in the frontier vineyard. The French maintained schools for the Indians but these schools did not follow the Spanish mission pattern. Schools for white children were usually attached to a parish, and the local priest was the teacher. There was some state support for schools, but there was really no school system as such. Judged in the context of the time and circumstance, these French institutions were well staffed. It is also difficult to see the origins of the present school system here. It is true that the French occupied a position of great influence in the early period of the history of the American hierarchy, but this was entirely dissipated by the latter half of the nineteenth century when the parochial school system was really formed.

The real origins of American Catholicism are in the English antecedents, not the Spanish or French. Because this is true, it does not necessarily follow that the origins of the parochial school system in the United States are Anglo-Catholic. The number of Roman Catholics in the thirteen British-American colonies was very small, perhaps thirty thousand or no more than two percent of the total population by the end of the Revolution. The Catholic population was unevenly distributed throughout the colonies. The heaviest concentration was in Maryland, Pennsylvania, Kentucky, southern Indiana, and Illinois. It was really in Maryland, however, that American Catholicity was born as that colony was established in 1634 explicitly to provide a haven for English Catholics. Even in Maryland, though, non-Catholics outnumbered Catholics. The typical colonist had little first-hand information about Catholicism or its adherents. Rossiter's observation was probably not far from the mark when he wrote:

> the Catholic occupied much the same position in colonial America that the Communist does today. Though few colonists had even seen or could have recognized a real live Catholic, they knew everything about the

Papists and shared a morbid interest in their doctrine and practice. They were also quick to brand people Papist who were not Papists at all. The press found Catholicism excellent copy, especially if the "facts" were bloody or erotic, and especially in times of war with Catholic Countries. Certainly the Catholic was feared with the same unthinking passion as the Communist is today. . . .[2]

Ignorance breeds fear, and fear begets repression. Probably only in Pennsylvania did Catholics enjoy anything approaching complete toleration. From 1664 to 1688, largely owing to the influence of James, Duke of York, who became James II in 1685, Catholics enjoyed a greater degree of freedom, but the "Glorious Revolution" of 1688 brought an end to this. The Anglican Church was actually established in Maryland, the home of Roman Catholicism in America. Jesuits were expelled from New York and also scattered in Maryland. Catholics were permitted to enroll as students in only two of the colonial colleges: the College of Philadelphia which was Quaker and the College of Rhode Island which was Baptist. Catholics found themselves in a more tense situation in periods when England was at war with a Catholic power such as France or Spain. After the outbreak of the War for Independence, Catholics benefitted from the alliance with Catholic France. Yet in the constitutions drawn up by the rebelling colonies as they became states, there was rarely a deliberate toleration of Catholics. The First Amendment of the United States Constitution did protect the freedom of worship from federal encroachments, but it did not prevent such infringements by the states. Indeed, some states continued the practice of supporting an established church for several decades after the Revolution. It was the Fourteenth Amendment as applied to the First by the courts that protected the freedom of religion from state meddling, but this was to come in a later era.

American Catholicism in the eighteenth century differed greatly from Catholicism in the nineteenth and twentieth centuries. In Maryland it was the religion of aristocrats. Certainly not all Catholics were wealthy planters of Anglo-Saxon origins; there were also a number of German and French Catholics in Pennsylvania and on the frontier who were mechanics or farmers. There were also miniscule traces of other ethnic groups such as the Poles. The number of Irish Catholics at this time was only a sprinkling. The real leadership in the Church throughout the colonial period and well into the nineteenth century remained in the hands of the old English Catholic group. This gave a complexion to the Church that it does not have today. The early Church fathers tended to be southern and agrarian in their point of view, and this was true, too, of their ideas on education. Catholics were a minority but they apparently were not extremely upset by the fact. In Maryland where they were most numerous, they occupied a high social status. Catholicism had not yet become the church of the immigrants. Catholic militancy was a characteristic of the Church only after enough Irish had immigrated to the United States to permit them to gain a strong voice in the Church. John Hughes, the Bishop of New York during the Civil War era, and John Carroll, the first Bishop of Baltimore, were completely different types of men and the flocks they guided were even more unlike. In many ways the Roman Catholic Church of the seventeenth century bears a stronger resemblance to the Protestant Episcopal Church of the post-Oxford era than it does to contemporary Roman Catholicism.

The educational activities of these British-American Catholics were at least as impressive as those of the Spanish and French. English Jesuits founded a school at Saint Mary's City in 1640. About 1673 a school was begun in Newton in Maryland which developed into Georgetown 116 years later—the oldest Roman Catholic secondary school for boys in the United States. In 1684 Governor Thomas Dongan, a Catholic, was instrumental in the establishment of a school in New York City at the corner of Broadway and Wall Street; a school had been operated there a short time by the Church of England. During the years immediately following the deposition of King James II in 1688, there was less public activity on the part of English-American Catholics with regard to schools.

One of the most famous schools of the colonial period was Bohemia Manor located in northeastern Maryland at the confluence of the Great and Little Bohemian rivers. Sometimes it was referred to as "Herman's Manor" because part of the property was originally owned by Augustine Herman. From the school grounds, one could see the Potomac River in the distance. Bohemia Manor was probably the epitome of the Jesuit school in British North America. It was a boarding school, and its curriculum appears to have been elementary and also college preparatory. Many of its students continued their studies at the Catholic college of Saint Omer in France or at other Catholic institutions on the Continent. It was a risky business for parents to support a school such as Bohemia Manor because after Catholics had lost control of the government of the colony, Catholic schools were made illegal in Maryland. In spite of this restriction youngsters still attended the school and in its heyday Bohemia Manor had an enrollment of about forty students. Judging from fragmentary records, the activities at Bohemia appear to have been sporadic, beginning in 1704 or 1706 or 1738 and continuing on to 1765 and maybe even after this. Sending a son or daughter to Europe was even more hazardous. The journey itself was long and dangerous. There was always the apparently greater possibility of contracting a fatal disease in Europe than in less congested and less polluted America. Parents might also entertain the legitimate fear that foreign schooling would unfit the child for life in the colonies. Furthermore, this was a rather costly enterprise. It was also illegal in Maryland to send a son or daughter to Europe for the purpose of acquiring Catholic schooling, but this was a hard law to enforce. John Carroll and Leonard Neale, both of whom would later serve as Archbishops of Baltimore, studied at Bohemia and then went abroad to round out their education. Interestingly enough, the last time John Carroll ever conferred the sacrament of Holy Orders was at the old Bohemia Manor.

The general state of education in colonial Maryland was low, and Catholic schools there were rather typical of southern education in general until the nineteenth century—a plantation schoolroom manned by a tutor or tutors and supported by a wealthy planter or planters. Education was, as a rule, available only to an elite who could afford it. It was considered the concern and responsibility of the parent. The low population density made a formal education for all an unattainable goal.

Philadelphia was the first instance of urban Catholicism in the United States, and in 1782 the first parochial[3] school was organized there in Saint Mary's Parish. The school plant constructed was probably as good as any in the country. Parish schools, of course, were not new with Saint Mary's; they were mediaeval in origin. The Church leaders at the Council of Vaison in Gaul in 529 had urged parish priests to maintain schools in their homes. Later at one of the Councils of Constantinople a similar decree was issued though it is a matter of conjecture just how well it was implemented. The fathers at the Council of Trent meeting in the middle of the sixteenth century ordered the reopening of parish schools wherever they had declined. Parochial schools were common in European countries such as France, England, and Germany. And it must not be thought that Roman Catholics were the only ones to continue the practice of establishing parochial schools in the thirteen colonies; Lutherans, Quakers, and Anglicans also founded them. Nowhere in the colonies, however, was there any group of schools organized into a system.

The first teachers at Saint Mary's school were lay Catholics. The first sisters' school was not established in the United States until 1801. The Philadelphia school was governed by a lay board of trustees. Male teachers taught the boys; and there were female assistants to instruct the girls. The curriculum appears to have been rather standard though, as was only to be expected, there was a strong dose of Catholic catechism.[4] Expenses were met in several ways. There were textbook and tuition fees. Some of the costs were covered by outright gifts, others from the Sunday collection plates. Lotteries were occasionally held to raise money for the Catholic school; this was an extremely common practice throughout the colonial period to raise funds for various activities. Certain wealthy Catholics also left endowments for the school in their wills. One such person was John Barry, "Father of the United States Navy." The practice of endowing schools was not unique to America or to Catholics. At least as early as 1653 a bequest for Catholic education was recorded in the colonies.

It is significant that there were several German Catholic schools in Pennsylvania at the time of the Revolution. German communities, even in the eighteenth century, showed a remarkable inclination to set up separate schools. This was true in non-Catholic as well as Catholic communities of German composition. There were possibly Catholic schools at Conewago, Sportsman's Hall, Carlisle, Milton, York, Taneytown, Frederick, Littlestown, Brandt's Chapel, Hanover, Lancaster, and Goshenhoppen. The last one, Goshenhoppen, was probably the most famous of the German parochial schools of the period. The Germans of Saint Mary's Parish of Philadelphia set up a new parish church of their own, Trinity Church, and built a school. This was an extremely interesting development as it harbingered the trustee crisis of the early nineteenth century and bore many characteristics of the German-Irish controversies of the latter nineteenth century. Some might well argue that if roots of the American Catholic parochial school system are to be found anywhere during this era they would be here in these more obscure German origins and not in the English and Jesuit enterprises in Maryland.

Immigration increased somewhat after the Revolution, and the Church increased in size though nowhere to the extent of the 1840's and afterwards. The number of Catholic schools likewise grew in the postwar years. In 1799 Visitation Academy—the first school for girls in what had been the thirteen colonies—was established at Georgetown. Yet the overall number of schools, by today's standards, remained very small. Perhaps seventy schools in all had been founded from the Maryland beginnings to the end of the Revolutionary era.

The American Church had long existed without the normal forms of ecclesiastical administration. Spanish enterprises had been directed through Cuba or Mexico, French through Quebec. The English Catholics along the Atlantic seaboard had had much less direction. The most significant religious community in the area in terms of numbers was the Society of Jesus. Between 1634, the date of the establishment of the proprietary colony of Maryland, and 1773 an estimated 186 Jesuits had served in the colonies. Virtually all of them served the colonies south and west of New England. Many of these men received their priestly faculties, that is, the official authorization of the Church to engage in active ministry, say Mass, and administer the sacraments, from the General of the Society of Jesus in Rome. Technically the colonies were under the jurisdiction of the Vicar Apostolic of London after 1688 who was really a missionary bishop. The colonies were regarded as mission territory, a status the United States would not lose in the eyes of the Vatican until the reign of Pope Pius X (1903–1914). The net result of all this was that priests functioned with much more independence than would normally have been the case. Community discipline in the Society of Jesus did give some greater semblance of order, and it also gave some degree of coherence to the schools they ran. However, on July 21, 1773 when His Holiness Pope Clement XIV issued the final decree *Dominus ac Redemptor* suppressing the Jesuits, much of this was lost; it was a backward step for the Church in America.[5]

There had long been discussion about the desirability of giving the American colonies a bishop of their own. After the Revolution the issue took on a sense of urgency. The Church was growing in numbers. A vast new territory had been guaranteed to the new nation by the terms of the peace treaty, and the Anglophobia developing from the war made the previous arrangement with the English Vicar difficult to maintain. It is interesting to note that the Anglican Church in America faced a similar difficulty, and it was at this time that Samuel Seabury and James Madison were consecrated bishops for the Protestant Episcopal Church in America. After the decision to create a Roman Catholic bishopric was made, the next problem was how to go about setting it up and whom to select for the position of first bishop. The Vatican chose to erect the first diocese in a series of steps over a period of years and named Father John Carroll the Superior of the American Missions in a letter dated June 9, 1784 from Cardinal Antonelli, Prefect of the Propaganda de Fide.[6] This was a temporary and preliminary step to the actual organization of the territory into a diocese. The final measure was taken in 1789 and announced by Pope Pius VI in the papal brief *Ex Hac Apostolicae* establishing the Diocese of Baltimore in Maryland and naming Father John Carroll the first Bishop of Baltimore.

Baltimore was a logical place for the center of the new see, and Carroll was a fine choice for Bishop. Carroll had been a Jesuit before the suppression of the Society in 1773. He was one of the Maryland Carrolls, an old, well-established Catholic family, and he was related to Charles Carroll, the signer of the Declaration of Independence. By the standards of any day, he was a well-educated man; he began his schooling at Bohemia Manor and completed his studies on the Continent. Carroll does not seem to have been the first choice of the American former-Jesuits for Bishop, but he was not an unpopular choice with his confreres. Carroll was known and respected by many prominent non-Catholic Americans, especially Ben Franklin who had recommended him highly to the Vatican when he was asked for his personal opinion of the priest. The property and funds with which the new diocese began operations had once belonged to the former-Jesuits. All things considered, the appointment of John Carroll was a fine one, possibly the best that could have been made. The Roman Church in the United States was fortunate to have his sober hand at the helm.

The episcopal powers can be conferred only by another bishop, and as there was none in the United States Carroll had to go abroad for his consecration. He decided to go to England rather than Rome or France. This decision, too, was a shrewd one. Bishops were, by the very nature of their office, suspect in low-church America. It would stir up a minimum amount of public reaction if the Pope or a "foreign" bishop were not involved in the ceremonies. It also reflects the English origins of the American Church at the time. On the boat to England with Carroll was Doctor James Madison who was soon to be consecrated the first bishop for the Protestant Episcopal Church in the United States according to the English Book of Common Prayer. Bishop Carroll and Bishop Madison also returned together.

On December 12, 1790, John Carroll formally took possession of his pro-cathedral[7] in Baltimore. For the first time since 1634 when Catholicity was brought to British America, there was a resident, native bishop for English-speaking Roman Catholics in North America. For 156 years the Church had not had a bishop. To appreciate how long a period of time this was, one might observe that it was not until 1946 that the American Church with its hierarchy had passed through as long a span of history. Like George Washington, Carroll was acting largely without precedent. When he acted and spoke, he did so with great deliberateness.

Bishop Carroll's views on education were rather typical of those of many Catholics of the time. In his first sermon upon his return from England he mentioned his concern "to devise a means for the religious education of Catholic youth—that precious portion of pastoral solicitude." Bishop Carroll convened a synod of the clergy under his aegis in 1791 to discuss some of the problems in the diocese. If the pastoral of 1792 is an accurate reflection of the discussions held, education was a topic that was considered. In his first pastoral letter issued in May, 1792, Carroll observed that parents and not the Church were the most important agents of religious formation. He urged parents to patronize the Catholic secondary school at Georgetown but candidly admitted that its relatively high tuition would put it beyond the reach of many.[8] What Bishop Carroll did not say is of interesting and significant note: there was no implication that every Catholic child should attend a Catholic school and there was no attempt to provide help for those who could not afford a Catholic school education. It is easy to read the present into the past, to see the origins of modern-day institutions in what has gone beforehand. Guilday wrote that "the conditions prevailing in Catholic life during the epoch (1790-1829) and more especially during Carroll's time hardly warranted placing the burden of a parochial school system upon priests and laity."[9] But this would seem to imply a misinterpretation of the educational sentiments of the time. It is true and must be remembered that the American Church was not in a position to subsidize the schooling of a large number of children: it was, after all, a mission church in the United States. But the early nineteenth century was still a period before compulsory, universal school attendance was widely accepted as a necessary goal. The idea that everyone should receive some formal education at whatever the cost had not yet gained general acceptance. This was the era before Andrew Jackson, before the Lancasterian experiments, before Horace Mann or Henry Barnard. John Carroll was a good priest and a fine bishop, but he was not a great educational trailblazer. Had the Church possessed the resources, it is still a moot point whether they would have been spent on the construction of a vast parochial school system.

This is not to say that Bishop Carroll was against parochial schools. On the contrary, he gave his personal blessing to the free school started in Emmitsburg, Maryland, at Saint Joseph's Church in 1810. It was the first of its kind to be run without charging any tuition, but it set no lasting precedent and always remained the exception to the general rule. This school was set up by Mother Elizabeth Bayley Seton, a convert to Roman Catholicism and foundress of the Sisters of Charity in the United States. Mother Seton was a personal friend of Carroll's and was a distant relative of Archbishop James Bayley of Baltimore and Presidents Theodore and Franklin Roosevelt.

In 1808 the Vatican split the Diocese of Baltimore into smaller suffragan dioceses and made Baltimore the metropolitical see, and Bishop Carroll, as a result, became Archbishop Carroll. Carroll died late in 1815 and was succeeded by the Coadjutor Bishop of Baltimore, Leonard Neale.[10] The new Archbishop was already seventy years old and lived only two years after his elevation. His successor was Ambrose Maréchal, a former professor at Saint Mary's Seminary in Baltimore. Maréchal was French; but the appointment of an American of French extraction was no surprise as French priests after the Napoleonic era were proportionally more numerous than the number of French laymen in the American Church.

Archbishop Maréchal made a visitation of the Baltimore Archdiocese early in his administration and filed a detailed report with the Propaganda de Fide on his findings in 1818. This provides an interesting commentary on the state of the Church and of Catholic education. Maréchal noted the existence of two Sulpician-run seminaries in the Baltimore Archdiocese. Connected to these was a college where, His Grace noted, Catholic and non-Catholic youth could avail themselves of the benefits of higher education. Maréchal also praised Georgetown which by this time had developed into a college run and staffed by the Jesuits who had been restored to favor in 1814 by the papal bull *Sollicitudo omnium ecclesiarum*. The Archbishop noted the pious work of various communities of nuns who provided convent schooling for girls and announced his intention to open free schools very soon in Baltimore for poor boys and girls regardless of their religious persuasion. This was praiseworthy but somewhat typical of the age; very often in early America where there were free schools, they were available only to the indigent. Opening Catholic schools to Protestants as well as Catholics was a practice that was not to be continued in the future. The Archbishop further registered his regret that many books and magazines being published were very anti-Catholic in their attitude. He also dwelt upon the need to provide funds to pay for the education of seminarians from families who were not in a position to underwrite the costs of such schooling by themselves. Archbishop Maréchal was a devoted pastor and seems to have appraised the American scene rather well, but he was not a Horace Mann in a Roman cassock.

During this period there appear to have been no papal writings or comments recorded directly pertaining to Catholic schooling in the United States. In 1800 His Holiness Pope Pius VII did state that children ought to be the first concern of bishops who should look after the quality of school teachers and school curricula, but these remarks, included in the encyclical letter *Diu satis*, were intended for the entire Church.[11] In 1824 Pope Leo XII stated that God was the origin of all true wisdom, but, here again, the remark was brief and very general. A year later Leo spoke out against antireligious books, a problem of grave concern to United States prelates, but his comments do not seem to have been prompted by their concern or by Maréchal's report of 1818.

Ambrose Maréchal died late in 1828 and was succeeded on the throne of Baltimore by James Whitfield, his personal choice for the position and his protégé. One of the first decisions Whitfield made as Archbishop was to convoke a provincial council.[12] There had been serious consideration given to the possibility of holding such a meeting since 1808 when Baltimore had been elevated to the status of a province, but political events in Europe prevented Carroll from acquiring the requisite permission of the Vatican. Leonard Neale had been too ill and on the throne for too short a period of time to arrange for such a conference. Maréchal had favored the meeting but delayed calling it for various reasons. Whitfield found that many of the preliminaries for the council were already underway when he took office. The meeting was held in October, 1829 in the cathedral in Baltimore. There were twenty-two persons in attendance representing approximately 600,000 Roman Catholics and a little less than three hundred priests.

The fathers at the Council of 1829 issued thirty-eight decrees, only a few of which were concerned with education. The first four decrees were devoted to the status of priests. Decrees five, six, seven, and eight were concerned with trusteeism.[13] Decree nine warned against the evils of using unapproved translations of the Bible, and this indirectly touched upon the school question. One of the most objectionable features of the public schools where they existed and of the Lancasterian schools was the employment of the King James Bible in their curricula. Decrees ten through thirty-two were taken up with ritual considerations such as the wearing of the biretta (a type of hat worn by priests), churching women, and the form of the baptismal ceremony. Decree thirty-three strictly forbade the use of unapproved catechisms and prayer books and proposed the preparation of an American Catholic catechism. The thirty-fourth decree stated that it was "absolutely necessary that schools be established in which the young may be taught the principles of faith and morality while being instructed in letters."[14] The next decree was concerned with the preparation of suitable school books. The two final edicts were devoted to the question of papal ratification of the first thirty-six articles and the convocation of another synod in three years. The Pope gave his official blessing on October 16, 1830.

Two pastorals were prepared pursuant to this conference. One was addressed to the clergy; the other, to the laity. The missive to the priests of the province was composed by Bishop England of Charleston. It was written in the most flowering rhetoric of the time and really stated very little about education other than to urge priests to watch over the instruction of the young.

The letter addressed to the laity reminded parents of their duties regarding the education of their children. In a warning to mothers and fathers the bishops said:

> How would your hearts be torn with grief did you foresee, that through eternity those objects of all your best feelings should be cast into outward darkness, where there is weeping and gnashing of teeth! May God in His infinite mercy preserve you and them from the just anticipation of any such result! But, dearly beloved, this is too frequently the necessary consequence of a neglected or improper education.

The bishops warned parents to be careful to show by their examples that they truly believed those things that they inculcated in their children. As for Catholic schools, the bishops concluded:

> How well it would be, if your [i.e., parents'] means and opportunities permitted, were you at this period to commit your children to the care of those whom we have for their special fitness, placed over our seminaries and our female religious institutions? It would at once be the best mode of discharging your obligations to your children . . .

Then there followed a denunciation of anti-Catholic books and periodicals.

This was an extremely important church conference, and the decree and letters were significant if only for their effect on later councils. Guilday has stated that the Council set "the norms of church discipline in the matter of education, namely, the establishment of a parochial school in each parish."[15] Burns saw the decrees as merely a legal recognition of an established practice, that is, the establishment of schools in each diocese.[16] The interpretation of Father Burns is more cautious, and it is probably closer to the truth. It is hard to read into these decrees, the first in the American Church ever to be enacted on the school question, anything even approaching the idea that there should be a school in every parish where every Catholic child should be in attendance. This was a sentiment that gained general acceptance fifty years later. The bishops at Baltimore in 1829 did not declare themselves in favor of universal schooling. Rather what they seem to have been saying is that when Catholic children go to school they should be able to receive training in faith and morals along with training in secular letters. This may or may not be possible outside of Catholic schools, but it would appear that the leadership in the Church did not consider it impossible at this time. "Non-Catholic" was not yet equated with "anti-Catholic." This would come very soon, but only after increased immigration and the onset of the Protestant crusade against Catholicism. Maréchal in his 1818 report to the Vatican had described the climate in the United States as very tolerant. The major dangers to the faith were, in his opinion, those from within the Church itself, not those from without.

The Council of 1829 did not command the erection of Catholic schools throughout the United States on a parish-by-parish basis. Nor did it require the integration of such schools into a diocesan system. Nor did it require attendance at such schools.

It would seem that the origins of the American Catholic parochial school system as a unique institution in world educational history do not rest in this period of history. One has to look for them sometime after the First Provincial Council of Baltimore of 1829.

* * *

That period of time in the history of the Roman Catholic Church in the United States spanning the colonial and very early national period might be viewed as an epoch and labelled the "Era of the English." The English ethnic group comprised the largest bloc in the American Church, and it almost completely dominated the machinery of government of the Church in that area that would become the United States. The influence of the Spanish and French was not so significant in this area, and the Irish and Germans were not yet so numerous.

The typical Catholics were southerners living in Maryland, Pennsylvania, or Kentucky. Unlike their counterparts of later generations, they were not urban dwellers. They tended to view education as a private concern with primary responsibility resting on the parents. Most of the schooling of the time was religiously affiliated; and Catholics, quite understandably, objected to any form of schooling that was anti-Roman Catholic. This was, however, the age before compulsory schooling, and the idea was not yet widespread that the State should provide a relatively free schooling for everyone. Catholic parents could send their children to Catholic schools, to non-Catholic schools, to no school at all, or could hire a tutor for their children. Probably very few Catholics received much formal Catholic schooling. The leadership in the Church did not view education very differently from the laity. It endorsed Catholic schooling as the ideal, but it does not seem to have envisioned any sort of all-encompassing Catholic school system with all Catholic youngsters in attendance. It is hard to see the origins of the Catholic parochial school system as it actually came to exist in this period of history.

NOTES

1. Religious orders and congregations are special societies in the Church, and their members are called "religious." Very often members of these religious institutes live together in a monastery or convent type of community which is governed by special rules and constitutions approved by Church authorities. Examples include Benedictines, Dominicans, Franciscans, Josephites, Jesuits, Christian Brothers, and Sulpicians.
2. Clinton Rossiter, *The American Colonies on the Eve of Independence* (New York; Harvest Books—Harcourt, Brace, and World, 1956), p. 89.
3. Technically speaking, this was not a parochial school since Saint Mary's was not a parish in the strict canonical sense of the term as the United States was not yet incorporated into a diocesan structure.
4. A catechism is a religious textbook containg questions and answers. Until recently, religion was often taught in a catechetical manner, that is, children were required to memorize specific questions and formula answers. One advantage of this approach that would have been significant in frontier America is that each child does not have to have a copy of the text.
5. Unless noted otherwise documents cited about the history of the Church in America are taken from: John Tracy Ellis (ed.), *Documents of American Catholic History* (Milwaukee: Bruce Publishing Company, 2nd ed., 1962) or *Documents of American Catholic History* (Chicago: Henry Regnery Company, 1967).
6. The Vatican office in charge of missions.
7. The official church of a bishop is called a "cathedral" because his "cathedra" or throne is housed there. A cathedral receives a special blessing not given to other ordinary churches. When a bishop uses a church that has not been so blessed, the church is then said to be "pro-cathedral."
8. Citations to pastoral letters written before 1919 are taken from: Peter Guilday (ed.), *The National Pastorals of the American Hierarchy (1792–1919)* (Washington, D. C.: National Catholic Welfare Council, 1923).
9. Peter Guilday, *The Life and Times of John Carroll, Archbishop of Baltimore (1735–1815)* (New York: Encyclopedia Press, 1922), p. 790.
10. Dioceses can be organized into a large administrative district or a province. The chief bishop of the province is an archbishop and that part of the province

NOTES

which he administers directly is called an "archdiocese" or "metropolitical see." A bishop of one of the other dioceses within the province is said to administer a "suffragan" diocese. An assistant bishop with the right of succession is a "coadjutor" bishop.

11. Unless a different citation is made, all references to papal writings are taken from: *Education: Papal Teachings* (Boston: Saint Paul Editions, Daughters of Saint Paul, 1960).
12. "Ecclesiastical councils are of four kinds: oecumenical or general; plenary or national; provincial; and diocesan. Though the word *Council* and *Synod* are synonymous, the term Synod is usually applied to the diocesan assembly. . . . A National Council is assembled by the express direction of the Sovereign Pontiff, who appoints an Apostolic Delegate to preside over the assembly in his name . . . A further delimination of the Council is that called Provincial, that is, an assembly composed of the archbishop and the suffragan bishops of a province. Seven Provincial Councils were held in Baltimore between the years 1829 and 1849. The seven assemblies are justly considered by American canonists as national in scope and authority, since the Archbishop of Baltimore was the sole metropolitan in the United States up to 1846. . . ." Guilday, *The National Pastorals of the American Hierarchy (1792–1919)*, p. xi.
13. The problem of trusteeism and the effects of the trustee controversy on Catholic education will be considered in the next chapter.
14. The standard history of the early Church Conferences is: Peter Guilday, *A History of the Councils of Baltimore (1791–1884)* (New York: Macmillan Company, 1932).
15. The standard source on the life of Carroll is: Guilday, *The Life and Times of John Carroll*.
16. The classic studies of the history of the Catholic schools are those by Father James A. Burns: *The Catholic School System in the United States: Its Principles, Origin and Establishment* (Chicago: Benziger Brothers, 1908) and *The Growth and Development of the Catholic School System in the United States* (Chicago: Benziger Brothers, 1912).

II
The Era Of The Irish
1829–1866

Whether the prelates meeting in Baltimore in 1829 realized it or not, the Roman Catholic Church in the United States was entering into a new era, one marked by unprecedented growth and change. The principal cause of these developments was the increasing flow of immigration from Europe. Until the Civil War era, many of the foreign-born coming into the country were from the United Kingdom—those from Ireland swelling the ranks of the Roman Catholic Church. It has been estimated that in the decade ending in 1830, 50,000 Irish had come into the country; in the decade ending in 1840, 207,000; in 1850, 780,000.[1] The peak year for Irish immigration was about 1851. As the Church grew in foreign-born membership, the older English-Catholic elite lost its control over the government of the Church to the newer Irish elements. More and more Irish-American bishops were being named to head American dioceses. The Catholic center of population was moving to the North although the cultural leadership remained in the South. The Irish were less satisfied with their minority status than had been the older English-Catholic group. As the Irish came more and more into the seats of power, the American Church became increasingly militant in defense of the faith. The Irish had had a long experience in defending their religion against what they considered English encroachments. The siege mentality that they had acquired over centuries in the Old Country could not be discarded overnight. Those coming to the United States between 1820 and 1860 were the contemporaries of Daniel O'Connell. It should not be surprising, therefore, that it was considered more honorable for Catholics to stand up and be counted.[2] The Irish tended to resent the older English core, and, within the Church itself, the attitude of the southern elite towards the newcomers was really very much akin to nativism.

Not only were the Irish more militant than their English-Catholic precursors, they tended to hold themselves aloof from their non-Catholic neighbors. This was the beginning of what might be termed the "Catholic ghetto." Few of the Irish came to America with any money, and as a consequence many of them settled in the East not far from their places of entry and took jobs in the factories of the growing cities. Roman Catholicism was losing its agrarian cast. Only a very few of the Irish came into the Middle West; and, then, they usually entered directly from Canada or came with the railroads as laborers. Not many went into farming; they lacked sufficient money and experience. It would be left to the Germans of the post-Civil War era to bring Catholicity to the farmlands of the Middle West.

The increasing number of immigrants, and among them Catholics, entering into the United States fanned the flames of xenophobia. Nativism took on the proportions of a crusade. In August, 1834, the burning of the Ursuline convent at Charlestown, Massachusetts, triggered a series of anti-Catholic activities that was to last at least two decades. A spate of pamphlet materials was printed by Catholics and non-Catholics to muster support for their positions. Perhaps the most famous of these was *Awful Disclosures* written by Maria Monk. Miss Monk was supposedly a former nun who had escaped from a Montreal convent. She told of subterranean passages connecting convents to rectories, of infants born from the illicit sexual relations of priests and nuns, of cisterns filled with dead babies, and of sisters smothered to keep them from revealing these awful secrets of the nunnery. Actually the authoress had never been a nun and died in jail in 1849 where she was serving a sentence for being a pickpocket and a prostitute. Still the book was a best seller. Some Americans became convinced that the Catholics were plotting to take over the Middle West. Unfortunately, the Church made things worse for itself by a series of blunders on the part of its leaders, namely, by the school fund controversy in New York, by some regrettable public utterances by various Church officials, and by the controversy over trusteeism. The leadership in the Church failed to appreciate the American milieu, something that was to happen more than once. Hard-handed tactics that may have been successful, even necessary, in Europe won only deep and lingering resentment in the United States—a fact that the old English-Catholic group had seemed to appreciate but the newcomers failed to grasp. The general population in America was better educated than that in Europe, and newspapers made local events into statewide or national news in a few days or weeks. Though the majority of the population was Protestant, the governments of the United States and of the various states were neutral and not anti-Catholic or anti-clerical as was the situation in many places in Europe.

The period of nativist agitation was also the era of the common school crusade. It was the time of Bronson Alcott, Ralph Waldo Emerson, James Gordon Carter, Henry Barnard, and, of course, Horace Mann. The public schools that were established were largely Protestant in orientation. Often times, parts of their curricula were legitimately objectionable to Catholics. For instance, one selection in an elementary school reader went:

> As for old Phelim Maghee, he was of no particular religion. When Phelim had laid up a good stock of sins, he now and then went over to Killarney, of a Sabbath morning, and got *relaff* by confissing them out o' the way, as he used to express it, and sealed his soul up with a *wafer,* and returned quite invigorated for the perpetration of new offenses.[3]

The use of the King James version of the Bible in public school classrooms was also of serious concern to Catholic parents. Many objected to the use of state funds for such blatantly sectarian purposes.

William Seward, a Whig and later a Republican, became Governor of New York in 1839, and he soon became concerned over the large number of Catholic children who were receiving no formal schooling because their parents considered the public schools too objectionable. There was as yet no comprehensive system of Catholic schools in New York, and those relatively few church-affiliated schools that did exist were sometimes too expensive for an immigrant family to afford. In his message to the legislature in Albany in 1840, Governor Seward proposed the sharing of state funds by public and non-public schools despite the private charter and religious affiliation of the latter. As should have been expected a bitter debate ensued over the relative merits of Seward's proposed program.

Bishop John Hughes of New York was the principal spokesman for the "Catholic position."[4] Hughes had been born in Ireland in 1797 and immigrated to the United States while in his teens. He attended school in Maryland where he studied for the priesthood. In 1826 he was ordained a priest for the Diocese of Philadelphia. Twelve years later he was named Coadjutor-Bishop[5] of New York. When that see was vacated in 1850, he was appointed to be Bishop; and, at the same time, the diocese was raised to the rank of archdiocese by the Vatican, and so Hughes, consequently, became the first Archbishop of New York. An excellent public speaker, a writer with a good journalistic style, a strong and forceful personality with a penchant for activism, and an intelligent and efficient administrator, John Hughes was ideally suited to the demands that his high office placed upon him. He reflected very well the Roman Catholic Church of his day as it was modified by the Irish influence. Hughes was an extremely controversial figure both within and without the Church. It may well be that controversy is a sign of influence; there is no debating the fact that the Archbishop was a man to be reckoned with. It was not surprising that Hughes stated his opinions on the school aid issue frequently, frankly, and forcefully. Many objected to a churchman's taking such an active role in a campaign for funds. Many, too, interpreted the Catholic position as an outright stand against the Bible. Arguments on both sides waxed intense and became increasingly intemperate, but Seward reiterated his position in January, 1841 and again in 1842. The legislature finally defeated his proposal and instead made New York schools more nonsectarian in nature. This, however, did not completely eliminate the objectionable reading of the unapproved versions of the Bible. Hughes quietly set about increasing the number of parochial schools in his diocese, but some Catholics were less willing to concede defeat. One priest, for instance, publicly burned several copies of the non-Catholic version of the Bible which had been distributed by Protestant societies to his parishioners. The whole New York episode was probably unfortunate. There was no real large-scale success in making the public schools neutral, and the bad publicity it engendered helped recruit enough new membership to keep the ranks of the anti-popery brigades filled for another generation.

A more serious school crisis developed in Philadelphia in the early 1840's. Bishop Francis Kenrick of Philadelphia was a more mild-mannered man than Hughes but nevertheless firm in his convictions. Francis Kenrick was also an Irish-born American. He was well educated, having finished his schooling in Rome. He was a more cosmopolitan man than Hughes, midway, one might say, between the former and someone like John Carroll. Kenrick was held in high esteem in Rome, and he would eventually become Archbishop of Baltimore. He took a keen interest in Catholic education in his diocese; and he made schools a priority though he would permit them to be constructed only on a firm financial footing. His brother Peter later became Archbishop of Saint Louis. Bishop Francis Kenrick was unsuccessful in his attempts to prevent objectionable Bible readings and religious practices in the public schools. The disagreement between Catholics and non-Catholics reached riot proportions in July of 1844. More than $250,000 worth of property was destroyed. Sixty persons were injured and forty were killed. Only the intervention of the state militia was able to quell these disturbances. By the end of the forties, American prelates such as Hughes and Kenrick seemed to have abandoned attempts to reach a rapprochement with the public school authorities, and, instead they increasingly supported the construction of more parochial-type Catholic schools. It should be noted that those parts of the country in which this was especially true were populated by immigrants. This was a phenomenon that would occur several times in the ensuing decades in other immigrant communities.

The rise of the common elementary school and the movement for compulsory education put the Roman Catholic bishops in a difficult position. Before this, prelates could assume that most education would occur in the home. What funds there were to be spent on education, therefore, could be devoted to Catholic colleges and seminaries. But with the rise of public schools the situation was changed. The alternatives were no longer a private education or no education; rather they were a private education, no education, or an inexpensive public school education. The latter was appealing to immigrants though it is true that most of them came to the United States with no deep-rooted loyalty to public education. The public schools were quite Protestant in orientation, and the bishops, namely Hughes and Kenrick, set out to make the public schools less objectionable to Roman Catholics. Failing in their attempts, they settled back and increased the support to private parish schools. This all took place between the years 1830 and 1855.

It is significant to note that Roman Catholic parochial schools began to multiply as the major Protestant denominations abandoned the parish school system in large numbers. Presbyterians, Congregationalists, Episcopalians, and others discontinued their efforts along these lines. The major exception, of course, was the Lutherans who were maintaining what was probably the largest private school network at the time, larger even than that of the Roman Catholics, about 240 separate schools by 1820. Today, as a result, excluding educational institutions supported by the Missouri Synod of the Lutheran Church and by Roman Catholics, Christian parochial schools are an exception to the general pattern. Many Protestants unfortunately failed to understand the Catholic position correctly and interpreted it as one of intractable opposition to public education. This had a catalytic effect. It helped to eliminate what hesitation there was on the part of some Protestants to support the public school movement, and it was a major factor in its eventual success.

The bad press which ensued from the trustee controversy was possibly as detrimental as that from the school and Bible issues. Before bishops had been appointed in the United States, a period of more than 150 years in duration, Catholic Church property was generally held by, and in the name of, a lay board of trustees. These men administered the property just as the lay boards did and still do in many Protestant churches. As the various areas of the country were incorporated into dioceses, the tendency was to transfer the property title to the bishop. Here and there some opposition was encountered, but the bishop eventually got his way and had the property put into his name. The problem was often complicated by ethnic considerations. In Philadelphia, for instance, in 1787, German Catholics separated themselves from Saint Mary's Parish and were incorporated as a new parish which they named Trinity. There was nothing in canon law to restrict lay trustees from controlling the physical administration of the parish plant. Canon law, however, does reserve the right to bishops alone to appoint and remove pastors. The crises in the trustee controversy were reached when lay boards insisted on selecting or dismissing priests. The height of the trustee controversy spanned the years 1780 to 1850, and the letters of bishops are replete with references to the problem. It is surprising that so many American Catholics today simply assume that Catholic parishes the world over are run in the same way as their own and that this has been true from time immemorial.

The most famous fight over a church title occurred in Philadelphia between the wardens of Saint Mary's Church and Bishop Conwell. An old and sick man, Conwell was unable to push the matter to a settlement, but his successor, Francis Kenrick, was able to force the trustees to submit to his wishes. In New York, Bishop Hughes wished to have church property transferred to his name but discovered that there were legal obstructions. He attempted to have them removed by the passage of a bill permitting ecclesiastical ownership of property, but all he succeeded in doing was to increase the ever-growing number of his enemies. Many Protestants considered the whole idea undemocratic and un-American — the people's property being taken over by one man appointed by Rome. A law was enacted making clerical ownership of church properties illegal in New York State. Fortunately for the Catholic Church, this law was never strictly enforced and was eventually repealed. Besides Philadelphia and New York, other major trustee disputes occurred in Baltimore (Maryland), in Charleston (South Carolina), in Norfolk (Virginia), in Atlanta (Georgia), and in Westmoreland County (Pennsylvania).

McAvoy writes that "there are many reasons why lay trustees attempted to take over the government of the newly organized Catholicism in the United States,"[6] but it might be said with as much accuracy that it was the bishops who were trying to take over. In most parts of the country, Roman Catholic laymen had preceded priests and bishops; and the clergy found a parish already organized when they arrived, though a parish in a non-canonical sense. There was a clergy shortage in the United States, and priests could not spend much of their time performing non-clerical duties; therefore, laymen filled in for them. Certainly, the Protestant practice of democratic church government had an influence on the Catholic minority.[7] Still another factor militating in favor of trusteeism was the small size of the typical parish. Some parishes in the 1970's have as many as ten thousand baptized members, but this was not at all the case in the 1830's when a parish would, at most, have had a few hundred. A parishioner could work in a parish actively and see more clearly than today the effects of his contributed moneys and services. Furthermore, the absence of state support for any sort of church-affiliated enterprise gave the trustee a lever he did not have in Europe. One reason then for the trustee controversy as it developed in America was simply that the American church warden saw more possibility of success. The nationalistic complexion that came to color the controversies was unfortunate and is too often overstressed by historians.

In 1822 His Holiness, Pope Pius VII, addressed himself to the problem of trusteeism and laid down four guidelines. He declared that only good men should serve as board members, that they could not deprive a pastor of his church or of his sustenance, that the ministerial functions of a priest did not come under the purview of the wardens' authority, and, finally, that trustees ought to be in consonance with the bishop. If legally possible, the bishop was to hold the title to the church property. The last will and testament of every bishop was to be made in duplicate, and one copy given to the witness of the signing of the instrument. Usually the bishop would designate that his property was to pass to the man duly appointed to be his successor.

These guidelines, as they came to be applied in the United States, made trusteeism a dead issue. Despite the sporadic opposition and setbacks to vesting legal title in the name of the bishop, the practice was generally accepted in the United States. As a result, most parochial schools in the country are now under the direct jurisdiction of the local bishop. This permits the chancery office to have a larger degree of control over Catholic schools than is the case of other denominational schools in which the parish boards of trustees own the schools. The organization of the parochial schools of the Roman Catholic Church into systems of schools on diocesan bases in the latter part of the nineteenth century could not have happened without this former development. For this reason, too, there are many similarities between all the Catholic schools in a given diocese. The system has worked well when the bishop has been an enlightened proponent of education, but when he has not, the quality of each school has tended to depend more on the local pastor. The tendency in the nineteenth century to select bishops from the area in which they were to serve had the effect of reinforcing this regionalism. It was, in a way, similar to the inbreeding that is supposed to occur when universities hire their own graduates for faculty teaching positions.

The anti-Catholic agitation of this period was, no doubt, intensified by the ever-increasing number of Catholic immigrants more than by the actions of persons like Hughes and Seward or by specific issues as trusteeism or Bible reading. It reached its climax by the late 1850's in movements like Know-Nothingism. Know-Nothingism was an anti-immigrant, anti-Catholic movement of the 1840's and 1850's. After 1852 it was an important political force in American society. Though officially called the American Party, it was popularly referred to as the Know-Nothing party because of the password "I don't know" used by members of secret lodges that were widespread throughout the country. The movement lost much of its vigor from in-fighting over the slavery issue and ceased to be a viable political force after 1856. By this time the major ideological outlines of American nativism had been drawn: anti-Catholic; anti-radical; and pro-Anglo-Saxon.[8] A decline in immigration and the approaching Civil War brought about a temporary truce. Men were needed to fill the army, and it was really immaterial where they were born or where they went to church if they were good soldiers.

The bishops were, to say the least, very concerned; and their pastoral letters reflected this interest. Meeting for a second conference in 1833, the bishops of the Province of Baltimore set up a committee to supervise the selection of suitable textbooks for use by Catholic children. There were to be three members on this panel: the presidents of Georgetown College, Mount Saint Mary's College at Emmitsburg, and Saint Mary's Seminary. Majority approval was needed for authorized use of any given text. The decision on textbooks was a sensible one; as was to be demonstrated by the New York controversy, anti-Catholic textbooks were, and long continued to be, a legitimate and serious source of grievance for Catholic parents. There was no objection to some of the widely used neutral textbooks of the day. Pike's arithmetic, Murray's reader, and Webster's speller were commonly used in the Catholic schools. The pastoral letter issued to the faithful at the end of the meetings was probably written by Bishop John England of Charleston, South Carolina. In it he stated the concern of the bishops for proper and adequate education of Catholic youth and noted that schools, colleges, and seminaries had been set up for boys and girls. "You are aware," he wrote in a remark intended for parents, "that the success and permanence of such institutions rest almost

The Era Of The Irish

exclusively with you." The pastoral was written in a rather elegant and flourishing style. It is interesting to note that England placed the ultimate success of Catholic schools on grass-root Catholic support, not on state aid; but this was 1833—only the beginning of the common school era—and it was not yet universally conceded that the state should support even public schools. The pressures from competing with an extensive system of publicly supported schools were not yet fully felt. Some state aid for Catholic schools had already been received in New York State between 1806 and 1824, and Hughes was working to get this program reinstated in 1840. Public aid would also be afforded to Catholic schools in Lowell, Massachusetts, for a seventeen-year period after 1835. Still public assistance for Catholic schools was an extreme rarity during this period, but then, many areas did not even have public schools. In addition to privately raised funds, Catholic schools began receiving aid from foreign mission societies, most notably from the Association for the Propagation of the Faith organized at Lyons, France, in 1822 and the Leopoldine Association for Aiding Missions headquartered in Vienna, Austria.

Meeting in Baltimore once again in 1837 for the Third Provincial Council, the bishops of the United States issued another pastoral letter, this one also written in the name of the bishops by the Most Reverend Doctor England. In it the bishops urged the faithful to support Catholic schools. "It is our most earnest wish," they continued, "to make them as perfect as possible, in their fitness for the communication and improvement of science, as well as for the cultivation of pure solid and enlightened piety." They also praised the work of the nuns. Compared to other pastoral letters of this period, 1829–1866, this is a rather lengthy statement, but only one paragraph in it is concerned directly with education. This is true of Church writings in general. Education, when it is mentioned at all, is treated in a few paragraphs or it is treated indirectly as, for instance, the comments of Pope Pius VII on trusteeism. The only major exceptions to this are the 1929 letter of Pope Pius XI and the *Declaration on Christian Education* issued by the fathers at the Second Vatican Council.[9]

The Fourth Provincial Council met at Baltimore in May, 1840, and again Bishop England was called upon to draft the pastoral. It was the last he would write. The "prosperity of religion" and "your salvation and that of your descendents" depend upon the kind of education given to your children, England wrote in a statement apparently intended for parents. He further observed that the faithful often patronized the schools by sending their children but sometimes failed to support them adequately which, one might suppose, was owing more to the straitened circumstances of the typical immigrant parent rather than to an unwillingness on their part to contribute financially to school support. It is erroneous, said England, to deprive a child of a Catholic education on the grounds that the youngster would profit more if presented with his tuition money in one cash sum after he was finished with his formal schooling and ready to embark upon adult life. It is an error, too, he felt, to save money by sending a child to an inferior school until the end of his education and then letting him finish in a better school. The Catholic schools in many areas were of such high quality, noted the Bishop, that some Protestant parents enrolled their children in them.[10] The bishops through this pastoral voiced their concern over the use of the Bible as an ordinary school book which, they felt, was the case in public schools. At the same time, they were very careful to state that they were in no way opposed to the teaching of the Bible or of church history in the classroom. They also stated their regret that the state of Massachusetts had failed to make restitution for the burning of the Charlestown convent and complained about the continuing problem of anti-Catholic textbooks. Praise was paid to the teaching sisters. One of the most significant statements made in the letter concerned the reasons for establishing Catholic parochial schools. The letter read:

> It is no easy matter thus to preserve the faith of your children in the midst of so many difficulties. It is not then because of any unkind feeling to our fellow-citizens, it is not through any kind of reluctance on our part, to contribute whatever little we can to the prosperity of what are called the common institutions of the country, that we are always better pleased to have a separate system of education for the children of our communion, but because we have found by a painful experience, that in any common effort it was always expected that our distinctive principles of religious belief and practice should be yielded in the demands of those who thought proper to charge us with error. . . .

This is probably the first printed mention of a school "system" by the American hierarchy. It was, to be sure, a "system" only in the loosest sense of the term; but it is significant because it indicates the deep commitment of the bishops to the practice of establishing Catholic schools as an alternative to public institutions. The historian Burns suggests that by this time, too, the laity were equally sold on the idea of a separate Catholic school system; if this were truly the case, it is hard to understand why admonitions to parents on the subject run through so many pastorals like a leitmotif. Other topics mentioned in the letter were intemperance, the problem of secret societies, and the turbulence stemming from the 1840 presidential campaign (Tippecanoe and Tyler Too!). The letter reveals a real concern on the part of the American hierarchy with the social conditions of the country. It is well written, and it is probably the finest that John England wrote. The most significant decree of the Council concerning education was that directing pastors from preventing Catholic children from using Protestant versions of the Bible, or participating in the recitation of non-Catholic forms of prayer, or joining in the singing of non-Catholic forms of hymns.

By 1840 there were about thirteen communities of religious women teaching in parishes. Between 1840 and 1861 twenty-five new religious communities entered the teaching field, including six brotherhoods. Most of these communities were European societies founding American branches. Many of the members did not speak English, but this presented serious problems only in exclusively English-speaking communities. In a German community, for instance, it was not thought so serious if the German nun up in the front of the classroom could not speak English. The typical parish school was only gradually becoming coeducational.[11] Originally, brothers and laymen taught the boys; nuns or laywomen, the girls. The grade schools were becoming coeducational and staffed almost solely by female teachers. This paralleled a similar trend in public elementary schools which were entering into the era of the schoolmarm. The reasons for this trend in the Catholic schools were several: fewer religious communities of men immigrated to the United States; the growth rate of male societies was less than that of convents; brotherhoods cost about twice the amount that a comparable number of nuns would cost a parish. By 1840 there were at least two hundred parish schools, still fewer than the number of Lutheran parochial schools; and more than half of these were now west of the Alleghenies, a further indication of the shift of the Catholic population center from the older southern core. The total Roman Catholic population was probably somewhere between 600,000 and 700,000 persons. There still was really no Catholic school "system" as such. Even in the public sector the organization of state-supported schools into integrated systems was just getting underway. The New York State legislature created the first state superintendency of schools in 1812, but the early history of the office was stormy and sporadic. The history of statewide organizations in Maryland, Ohio, and New Hampshire—pioneering areas in school administration—were very much the same. Gideon Hawley, the great pioneer in the area of professional school administration in New York, had no contemporary counterpart in Catholic education. What organization and administrative integration there were in Catholic educational institutions at this time was owing more to the character of individual teaching communities than to any diocesan or provincial plans.

The Fifth Provincial Council met in the metropolitan capital of Baltimore in 1843. The bishops in the ensuing pastoral reminded parents once again of their obligations to teach their children their religious faith and lamented the sectarian orientation of the public schools. It is a "natural right" of parents, said the bishops, that their children be educated in the public schools without any interference with their religious beliefs or practices. Obviously the idea that every Catholic child must attend a Catholic school was not yet completely accepted. The Pastoral Letter of 1846 issued pursuant to the Sixth Provincial Council of Baltimore was unusually short and most remembered as the occasion on which the bishops made Our Lady of the Immaculate Conception[12] the national patroness and designated her feast day on the church calendar as a special holy day throughout the United States. The last provincial meeting of the Baltimore Archdiocese to legislate for the entire United States was the Seventh Provincial Council of 1849.[13] The letter the bishops then approved for distribution to the laity dealt at length with the problems confronting the papacy and with the doctrine of the Immaculate Conception. It did not treat of education at all.

The bishops at the provincial meeting at Baltimore in 1849 had reacted favorably to a suggestion that a national synod be held in 1852. The Holy Father, Pope Pius IX, approved the plan in 1851 and named the Archbishop-Designate of Baltimore, Francis Kenrick, to preside over the meeting in his name. The First Plenary Council was attended by approximately six archbishops and twenty-six bishops, representing a Catholic population of perhaps 1,600,000 persons. Significantly, not one of the archbishops in attendance was a native-born American. Twenty-five decrees were issued by the members of the Council, and these became binding when approved by the Pope. Bishops were urged to set up regular parish lines for priestly jurisdiction. Furthermore, bishops were urged to set up parish schools. The text of the decree on schools read:

> We exhort the bishops, and, in view of the very grave evils which usually result from the defective education of youth, we beseech them through the bowels of the mercy of God, to see that schools be established in connection with all the churches of their dioceses; and, if it be necessary and circumstances permit, to provide, from the revenues of the church to which the school is attached, for the support of competent teachers.

Titles of ownership of church properties were to be transferred to the local bishop to prevent further trustee scandals. Priests were to guide personally the catechetical instruction of youth, and a serious effort was to be made to secure a German language catechism to be used in Catholic schools in addition to the English language catechism then in use. This reflected the growing numbers of German immigrants swelling the ranks of the laity in the United States, but the Church at this time was still firmly in the grasp of Irish Catholics and would continue to be for at least another generation.

The Pastoral Letter of 1852 issued after the sessions of the First Plenary Council was written in the name of the bishops of the United States by Archbishop Kenrick of Saint Louis, brother of the Apostolic Delegate and Archbishop-Designate. The letter closely paralleled the decrees of the Council, and it contained a warning to parents to take special care in the education of their children in order to protect them against "all the evils of an uncatholic education. . . ." Children should be taught the "science of the saints" at the same time they are instructed in "human science," declared the bishops. "Listen not," they continued, "to those who would persuade you that religion can be separated from secular instruction."[14] The bishops urged parents to support Catholic schools in what was possibly the strongest exhortation on the subject to date, and they noted the fact that these admonitions reflected the sentiments of the Pope.

One year after these plenary sessions, in 1853, the Roman Court decided to have a personal representative of the Holy Father pay an official visit to the United States. It was a decision that reflected either heroic bravery or much naivete, more likely the latter. It was not a wise decision to put so visible a symbol of Roman Catholicism on public display. It exacerbated the anti-Catholic elements of nativism already operating at a feverous pitch in many parts of the country. Pope Pius IX had enjoyed a modest degree of popularity in the United States for a short period of time immediately after his elevation in 1846 when he appeared to be somewhat liberal in his administration of the Papal States; but what, if any, liberal trappings the Pontiff had had were gone by 1853 and so was the modicum of popularity he had possessed in Protestant America. Archbishop Gaetano Bedini, who was enroute to Brazil where he was to assume the duties of Diplomatic Nuncio, was appointed to be the delegate. He was to tour the United States and report on the state of Catholicism there directly to the Holy Father in Rome. The historian DeCourcey, a contemporary of Bedini, in his analysis of the visit stated that it was set up "in order to make America better known at Rome, and also to make Rome better known in America."

It should be noted that the American hierarchy was not even consulted about the visit, but rather it was merely informed of it by a letter sent from the office of the Congregation of the Propaganda in Rome. The American Government was informed of the visit about two weeks before the bishops were notified. The arrival and tour of the Archbishop sparked a wave of riots that continued for nearly a year. The visit, to say the least, was unfortunate. It was an instance where the Vatican failed to appreciate the American milieu, something that happened more than once.

Bedini in his official report to the Holy See did discuss a few of the problems confronting Catholic educators. He noted the great sacrifices that Catholic parents had to make in order to support separate schools without any kind of state aid. He noted, too, the tremendous amount of power held by American bishops. This was owing largely to the fact that in a mission country, which is what the legal status of the United States was in the eyes of the Vatican, bishops were not checked by strong cathedral chapters. Pastors of parishes could be removed at the will of the bishop and did not have a permanent position with tenure as they had in nonmission countries. Bedini did not comment on one important result: this characteristic of the American Church tended to make the number and quality of parish schools vary from diocese to diocese depending on the local bishop. Archbishop Bedini commented on the nationalistic tendencies of the newly arriving German Catholics, and he rather astutely predicted a division in the ranks of the Church between German and English-speaking Catholics. Too often Catholic historians have decried the kind of treatment Bedini received in the United States but have failed to consider the general advisability of such a state visit as an act of diplomacy in the context of the times. The information that the Vatican received from the Bedini tour could doubtlessly have been obtained in better ways. The anti-Catholic sentiments it generated certainly did nothing to ameliorate the plight of the Catholic child in the public school or of the Catholic school in a predominantly Protestant society.

There was no national synod of the American hierarchy from 1852 through the Civil War era. The bishops met again in plenary conference in 1866 after the conclusion of the war. Compared to the actions of the episcopal conferences of the preceding forty years, little was done by way of school legislation. All that was really accomplished was a restatement of earlier positions and decrees. Bishops once again urged pastors to build and equip schools and directed that regular catechetical instruction be arranged for those attending public schools. There was also a statement in the decrees concerning the erection of a Catholic University of America. This was the great dream of Martin John Spalding who was Archbishop of Baltimore (1864–1872) and who was presiding in the name of the Pope at the Second Plenary Council in 1866. The Catholic University of America was not founded, however, until the 1880's.

The pastoral letter reflected the content of the decrees. It was rather short considering the important nature of the meeting and the fact that no similar meeting had been held in the previous fourteen years. It contained the usual requests for support and patronage and praised the work of the various teaching religious communities. The bishops, however, did stress the need for Catholic vocational institutions and correctional schools. Delinquency, it would appear, is a problem most acute in poor, congested, urban areas. In many of the great northern cities of the mid-nineteenth century, the city ghettoes were largely inhabited by immigrants. This put a special burden on the Church as a disproportionately large percentage of the youths in state correctional institutions were Catholics. Hence, this statement was inserted in the Pastoral Letter of 1866. The bishops also noted the problems resulting from the manumission of the slaves in the South and declared that there was a need to provide the Negro with a Christian education. The Church never achieved great success in this field, however, for several reasons: the low Catholic population density in the South; the Church's necessary preoccupation with the Americanization of Catholic immigrants in the North and East; and the understandably human tendency on the part of many unskilled immigrants to view the blacks as job competitors. Ironically, there was also a tendency on the part of blacks to view immigrants as job competitors. Traces of this anti-immigrant feeling can be seen in the writing of Booker T. Washington.

Without doubt, one of the most interesting as well as puzzling passages of the Pastoral Letter of 1866 was the suggestion that parents consult their means as well as their wishes. By this the bishops apparently were not referring to the choice between a public or a Catholic school as they exhorted parents to patronize Catholic institutions. Rather what the bishops seem to have been referring to was the content of the secondary education to be received. "Prepare your children," said the bishops, "for the duties of the state or condition of life they are likely to be engaged in: do not exhaust your means in bestowing upon them an education that may unfit them for their duties." This statement would almost seem to harken back to the Maryland era of American Catholicism. It reflected a belief in the wisdom of an appropriate rather than an equal education for all. It is more Jeffersonian in philosophical viewpoint than Jacksonian. It is somewhat like the position taken by Booker T. Washington in the Atlanta Compromise of 1895. It is really not possible to tell what inspired the insertion of this passage, but the intended reader would appear to be the immigrant parent. Again, it would be hard to say what kind of impact this passage had on parents debating whether to send their children on to secondary schools and colleges—probably not very much. Interestingly enough, even today, contrary to the sentiments expressed by the bishops, there are Catholic high schools that accept students from varying backgrounds and of differing abilities but offer no vocational or industrial programs in their curricula.

Just as the years spanning the period from the First Provincial Council of Baltimore (1829) to the Second Plenary Council of the United States (1866) were eventful ones in the history of American Catholicism, they were not without milestones in Rome. Pope Pius VII had died in August of 1823. After the collapse of an uneasy settlement with the French, he had been taken a prisoner by Napoleon. Pope Pius had been prevailed upon to restore the Society of Jesus in 1814. He was succeeded on the throne by Pope Leo XII whose five and one-half years on the Chair of Saint Peter were less turbulent. Leo was followed in March, 1829 by another Pius, but Pope Pius VIII lived only a year and a half after becoming Pontiff. His successor was Gregory XVI. Pope Gregory's tenure was not especially remarkable. He died in June of 1846 after a term in office of fifteen years. The next Pope, however, was destined to leave quite an impression upon the Church. Pope Pius IX who was elevated in 1846 served for thirty-two years, one of the longest reigns in the history of the papacy. All of these men were Italians. None of them had ever been to America. Their knowledge of the United States was secondhand and seems to have been quite cursory. No important American prelate held a high position on the Curia. It is extremely doubtful that there were more than a very few in the Roman Court who could read English.

These popes wrote and said little directly concerned with education and virtually nothing regarding American education. What they did say that has been recorded is very homiletic in nature, rather abstract and general in application. Much of it was by way of allocutions to visitors and pilgrims or letters to various bishops—almost all addressed to Europeans, more precisely to Italians. A rather typical statement, by way of example, is that of Pope Gregory XVI made in a letter dated June 21, 1836 praising the Congregation of the Secular Clergy of the Schools of Charity. "Nothing can be of greater benefit to both Christian and civil society," wrote the Pope, "than a timely formation of youth in piety and civil virtue." This statement, like most of those made by the popes on education, is brief and really offered nothing that the American bishops could refer to as a guideline to the solution of some of the unique educational problems facing them in the United States. There is only one explicit reference in the American pastorals of the period to papal teachings on education, the brief paragraph in the Pastoral Letter of 1852 noting that Pius IX urged Catholic bishops to look after the religious instruction of young people.

What the popes said regarding education, when they said anything at all, was quite traditional. It is doubtful that the American bishops were conversant with anything but the major encyclicals and constitutions; but in light of the content of the minor statements, it does not seem to have really mattered. The lag in communications gave the American hierarchy some slight degree of independence. The Vatican, too, was quite preoccupied with the political situation in Europe and in the Papal States with the reverberations of the Treaty of Vienna of 1815 which manifested themselves in waves of revolutions in Europe that lasted nearly sixty years. That the popes of the nineteenth century said far less about education than their twentieth-century counterparts may be owing partially to this factor, partially to inferior means of communication and recording, and to less frequent audiences and public appearances. Certainly the general interest in education was increasing as the nineteenth century blended into the twentieth.

The most significant papal statements of the period on education were those of Pope Pius IX. In 1847, one year after his accession, he wrote that "the Sacred Congregation [of Propaganda] is not blind to the importance of giving scientific instruction to youth, especially youth of the higher classes." Apparently the Pope subscribed to the belief in an education appropriate to one's social and economic status. This idea was similar to that expressed by the American hierarchy in the Pastoral Letter of 1866 which was noted earlier. This philosophy was not new; it was older than the Greeks. There is no reason to suppose that the American bishops were inspired by this papal statement. Indeed, it is doubtful that they were aware of it.

In an encyclical letter addressed to the bishops of Italy, Pius told the prelates that it was their duty "to supervise all public and private schools and to study and labor to ensure that the program of studies agrees with Catholic teachings on all points." This was easier done in Catholic Italy than in the United States, but an Instruction to the Nunciature in Paris of the following year had more application to the American milieu. The Pope noted that the Church was prepared to endure some things opposed to its teachings if they did not endanger the existence of the Church and if this toleration made the position of the Church in society less difficult. Ordinarily, wrote the Pope, the Church would favor separate schools for Catholic children.

In a letter dated January, 1858, Pope Pius noted that "the prosperity of the State depends in great measure on the proper education of Christian youth."[15] His Holiness felt that many of the contemporary problems facing the society in which he lived stemmed from the removal of religion from public education. The removal of public and private education from the control of the Roman Catholic Church is the "greatest misfortune" of society. The Pope equated "Catholic" with "Christian" which, although not ecumenical, was logical in the light of his condemnation of indifferentism or the belief that one religion is as good as another.

The most controversial pontifical statement of the period, and quite possibly of the past five hundred years was the *Syllabus of Errors* issued on December 8, 1864. It was issued as part of a jubilee observance honoring the Pope, but it had been thirteen years in preparation. Vincent Cardinal Pecci was probably the first to suggest such a document to the Pope. Cardinal Pecci succeeded Pius on the throne in 1878 as Leo XIII and ironically has been considered by many to have been a liberal because of his labor encyclical *Rerum Novarum*. The *Syllabus* was really nothing other than an anthology of earlier condemnations made by the Pontiff. As Archbishop Spalding noted, the condemnations appeared especially ferocious when read out of the original context in which they had been intended. The *Syllabus* was a victory for ultramontanism, a nineteenth-century movement in the Catholic Church that was extremely conservative in viewpoint. The typical ultramontanist favored increased dependence upon the Holy See in matters of faith and morals. The ultimate victory for the movement, of course, was the 1870 declaration on papal infallibility. Most ultramontanists strongly favored the *Syllabus*. From the American point of view the *Syllabus* was unfortunate. It was a regressive document and had only a very limited application to the American situation. Few ultramontanists could appreciate the fact that the American culture while not pro-Catholic was not anti-Catholic. Pius was preoccupied with the problem of State encroachments on the rights of the Church. Because American Catholics were forced to support their own churches and schools did not mean that the federal and state governments were opposed to such institutions. The *Syllabus* contained condemnations of the belief that education ought to pertain to the State alone, a tenet that was not widely accepted in the United States. It was also condemned to hold that "Catholics may approve of this system of educating youth severed from the Catholic faith and the power of the Church, and which regards the knowledge of merely natural things, and only, or at least primarily, the aim of earthly social life." But this too was not a characteristic of nineteenth-century American thought on education. Like the Inquisition or the treatment of Galileo, the *Syllabus of Errors* has been a source of embarrassment to many American Catholics.

* * *

The forty-year period of American Catholic history spanning the years 1830 to 1870 might be viewed as an epoch and labelled the "Era of the Irish" just as the period before 1830 might well be called the "Era of the English." Of course, tags such as these are artificial devices of the historian, but they do serve a useful purpose if they are not interpreted too rigidly. The forty-year period in question was marked by an immense wave of immigration. Most of the Catholic newcomers up to the Civil War were Irish. In the minds of many Americans "foreign" and "Catholic" became synonyms. As the Irish settled in the cities of the North and East, the population center and the leadership of the Church passed from the older southern English-Catholic core. This older elite group viewed the new arrivals with disdain and did not surrender the seats of power willingly, but sheer numbers were against them.

This same forty-year period was also the era of the common school movement. The lure of free schools, many of which were anti-Catholic in nature, presented a problem to the American hierarchy. At first they attempted to make these schools less hostile to Catholicism. Failing in this attempt, they turned to a device already used in America by many religious groups, a device as old as the Middle Ages—namely, the parochial school. Judging from the pastorals and decrees of the bishops' meetings of the period, the consensus of opinion of the American hierarchy was that separate Catholic schools were desirable; and they urged bishops to encourage them, pastors to build them, and parents to support and patronize them. Parochial schools were encouraged, and encouraged strongly: they were not made mandatory. There was as yet no parochial school system. Each parish school was rather autonomous. One important difference between the parochial schools of this period and those of the "English Era" should be noted. Before the common school movement, a parish school was often the only school available. During the "Irish Era" the parochial school was an alternative means of education.

The great centers of the parochial school movement during the early part of the period were New York and Philadelphia, and the early champions were the Irish. It would be difficult to determine whether the Irish built these schools primarily as Irish Catholics or as Irish immigrants. One would suspect as both; but, perhaps, a little more as the latter. As the Irish became more Americanized, they seemed to become less enthusiastic in their support of separate schools. After 1870, the Irish were definitely less enthusiastic than the Germans in their support of separate Catholic schools. These institutions were originally established for two motives: one was religious, the other—to protect the foreign subculture—was not. The "Irish culture," though many Irishmen would become irate at the suggestion, is really a variant of the English as is the "American culture." The Irish immigrant in many ways did not have as many adjustments to make as did non-English-speaking latecomers. The official documents of the American hierarchy really reflect none of this.

The pontifical writings of the period on education were few in number, rarely available in English, and directed more toward the political, economic, and social makeup of the European continent. They appear very unimportant in the history of American Catholic education.

Possibly the most significant development of the period was that American Catholics acquired the parish-school building habit. The Germans would make this habit mandatory.

NOTES

1. Gerald Shaughnessy, S.M., *Has the Immigrant Kept the Faith? A Study of Immigration and Catholic Growth in the United States, 1790–1920* (New York: Macmillan, 1925), p. 79.
2. George Shuster summed this up rather well when he wrote: " . . . the Irish immigrant was a great deal closer to Queen Elizabeth and the Spanish Armada than he was to the Second Vatican Council." *Catholic Education in a Changing World* (Chicago: Holt, Rinehart and Winston, 1967) p. 29.
3. Quoted in Neil G. McCluskey, S.J. (ed.), *Catholic Education in America: A Documentary History* (New York: Bureau of Publications, Teachers College, Columbia University, 1964), p. 71n.
4. It would really more correctly be termed "the position of many Catholics."
5. A "coadjutor" is an assistant bishop. Unlike an "auxiliary" who is also an assistant bishop, a "coadjutor" usually has the right of succession when the see becomes vacant.
6. Thomas T. McAvoy, *A History of the Catholic Church in the United States* (Notre Dame, Indiana: Notre Dame University Press, 1969), p. 93. Father McAvoy's book is probably the finest one-volume history of the Church in America. His interpretations are revisionist in many aspects. A more standard interpretation of the history of the Church is: John Tracy Ellis, *American Catholicism* (Chicago: University of Chicago Press, 1956).
7. A fascinating nineteenth-century account of the history of the Church is: Henry DeCourcey, *The Catholic Church in the United States* (New York: Edward Dunigan and Brother, 1856). DeCourcey, a contemporary of the trustee crises, wrote that "the Catholics in the United States, living amid a Protestant population, and influenced by surrounding ideas of independence have not always shown the subordination ever to be desired toward pastors. The temporal administration of the churches is the source of constant collisions; and the laity, seeing the manner in which Protestant churches are managed, frequently usurp powers not their own."
8. John Higham, *Strangers in the Land: Patterns of American Nativism, 1860–1925* (New York: Atheneum, 1969), pp.3–11.
9. These two documents will be discussed further in subsequent chapters.
10. This is a very interesting revelation. Pope Pius XI, writing almost a century later, in 1929, inveighed against what he called "mixed schools," that is, schools where Catholic children were educated in common with non-Catholic children. The Catholic schools of the 1830's were, therefore, being run as "mixed schools," or else the definition of "mixed school" should be further defined as a school in which non-Catholic and Catholic children are educated together under non-Catholic auspices. *Encyclical Divini illius Magistri* (Christian Education of Youth), in *Seven Great Encyclicals* (Glen Rock, New Jersey; Paulist Press, 1963), p. 60.
11. It is interesting that these schools were becoming coeducational. Pope Pius XI in his 1929 encyclical *Divini illius Magistri* expressed strong disapproval of co-education but this aspect of his letter was virtually ignored in the United States.
12. The Immaculate Conception reflects the traditional Catholic belief that by special divine privilege Mary was conceived and born without original sin.
13. After this time there was more than one archdiocese in the United States, and so the decisions reached at Baltimore affected only part of the country.
14. This last warning is especially interesting in that many of today's proponents of public aid to Catholic schools argue just the opposite, namely, that some subjects are wholly secular and should, therefore, be subsidized from government coffers.
15. This, surprisingly enough, is quite similar to an idea expressed by Horace Mann who wrote: "The truth has been so often asserted that there is no security for a

NOTES

republic but in morality and intelligence, that a repetition of it seems hardly in good taste. . . . I know we are often admonished that, without intelligence and virtue, as a chart and compass, to direct us in our untried political voyage, we shall perish in the first storm; but I venture to add that, without these qualities, we shall not wait for a storm—we cannot weather the calm. . . . Unless these qualities pervade the general head and heart, not only will republican institutions vanish from amongst us, but the words prosperity and happiness will become obsolete." *Lectures and Annual Reports on Education* (Cambridge, Massachusetts: Published for the Editor by the Cornhill Press of Boston, 1867), p. 151. Gerald Lee Gutek notes that "although liberal in his theology, Mann recommended the teaching of a 'common Christianity' in the public schools." *An Historical Introduction to American Education* (New York: Thomas Y. Crowell, 1970), p. 54.

III
The Era Of The Germans
1866–1919

There was an unspoken moratorium on anti-Catholic activities during the Civil War. Applied bigotry is a luxury that one can afford only in peace time and in periods of relative prosperity. Not that the enmity between many Catholics and non-Catholics did not exist during the war but rather it was not so manifest. The waves of immigration that had been greatly reduced by the outbreak of hostilities resumed in full strength almost immediately at the war's end.

By 1870 the anti-popery brigades were active once with no less a figure than President Ulysses Grant taking part. He publicly supported an amendment to the federal Constitution that would have required attendance of all children at public schools and denied any kind of aid whatsoever to religious institutions. Grant's motives, like Seward's in the 1840's, are subject to speculation. He may have been speaking his conscience, but then again it was 1875 and the Republican Party was only a year from the photofinish race to the White House between Tilden and Hayes. It was, perhaps, a gauge of the times that the measure was defeated only by a narrow margin. Even a person of the background of Richard Henry Dana[1] denied the right of Catholic parents to object when their children were compelled to read the "Protestant Bible." Grant's position differed from Dana's only in degree.

Representative James Blaine had introduced the Grant-favored amendment in Congress in 1875. Thirteen years later Senator Henry

The Era Of The Germans

Blair unsuccessfully championed another very similar proposal for a constitutional amendment. It too received a good deal of support but not enough to be enacted. The idea that all children should attend a public school was raised now and again until 1925 when the United States Supreme Court ruled that a 1922 law enacted by the legislature of the state of Oregon making mandatory the attendance of all children in a public school was unconstitutional.[2] The right to existence of Catholic parochial schools was finally guaranteed in law. The decision seems logical when viewed in retrospect, but it was also expedient in light of the vast investment in Catholic school properties by that time.

During the first great wave of Catholic immigration in the 1840's and 1850's, the movement for public schools was really just getting under way. Many immigrants had no strong commitment to formal schooling. Bishops in office from 1870 on, that is, during and after the second period of mass Catholic influx, found themselves in a different position from that of their predecessors. The idea that every child should have some formal schooling was gaining increased general acceptance in the United States, and many state legislatures were enacting compulsory attendance laws. During the "Era of the English," the choice facing parents would often have been a denominational school or no school; during the "Era of the Irish," a denominational school, an inexpensive public school, or no school. With the enactment of laws requiring attendance of all children at school the last option was removed; the choice now confronting many parents was a parochial school or an inexpensive public school. This put many Catholic parents in something of a dilemma. They wanted their children to receive the benefits of a formal education either because of personal commitment, social pressures, or legal requirements but many still strongly objected in conscience to the public schools. Public school authorities were rarely willing to make concessions for minority groups because they feared this would retard the "Americanizing" process. Whereas bishops once could spend the bulk of their resources on colleges and seminaries, they had now to expend increasing amounts to meet the demands for Catholic elementary schooling.

The Germans were the most numerous of this second wave of mass immigration, their crest being reached about 1882. Nearly 1,500,000 Germans entered into the United States in the decade beginning in 1880. It has been estimated that approximately 5,500,000 Germans came to the United States between 1820 and the passage of immigration-restriction laws in the 1920's. More immigrants came from Germany than from any other country. The Irish were the second largest immigrant group. Out of a total Catholic population in the United States of approximately 9,000,000 souls in 1890, perhaps as many as 4,750,000 were of Irish stock — or slightly more than half of the total, and the number of German Catholics was about 1,900,000. The reason that the percentage of German Catholics was not higher after the great influx of immigration was owing to a high mortality rate and to the fact that many Germans were Lutherans or Calvinists. There is no circumventing the fact, however, that the Germans were a large minority bloc in the Catholic Church, and they exercised an even greater influence on the policy-making centers of the Church than their roughly twenty percent of the Catholic body politic would warrant because they tended to settle in very compact, self-contained communities. Many of them settled in the Midwest, and there developed a triangle of German settlement extending from Milwaukee down to Saint Louis and east to Cincinnati.

The Germans were especially willing to establish parochial schools.[3] They were the leading school builders and were more inclined to develop them than their Irish confreres though the latter were certainly no enthusiasts for the public schools. There were several reasons for this phenomenon. The Irish immigrants were, on the whole, poorer than their German counterparts; they did not have the money to pay for an extensive school system. The Irish spoke the same language as the dominant majority in the United States, and, furthermore, their culture, if they did indeed have one that was truly distinct from the English, was not so distinct from that of mainstream America as was that of the Germans. Some persons alleged that these Germans were more interested in preserving their subculture than in protecting the faith, and if the high ratio of lay teachers to religious faculty is any indication of this, then it was certainly true. The German brought a rich educational heritage with him to the United States. Germany was a great pioneer in the common school movement. By the end of the eighteenth century regular school attendance was required by law; an orderly system of school supervision and of teacher certification had been set up, free schooling was provided for the poor, and religious as well as secular instruction was included in the regular school curriculum. Prussia was one of the first states to advance the doctrine that the government's authority in education is paramount, and the German immigrant, from his past experience, tended to be wary of what he considered State encroachments on the prerogatives of the Church and family. He was also accustomed to the utilization of public funds for religious instruction. In the United States, private schools had a much freer reign, but the State was not disposed to giving them public assistance.

The Irish and the Germans were both concerned with being "Americanized," that is, being assimilated into or accepted by the mainstream of American culture. Unlike the Germans, however, the Irish did not view the event with great alarm. This, too may have been a reason why they were less concerned about the need for establishing parochial schools. The social standing of the classmates that their children would encounter in the parish school was often not so high as that of children in public schools, and foreign nuns were sometimes viewed as a very definite liability. By this time, too, many of the public schools were well on their way to becoming less objectionable to Catholics. If they were not yet truly secular, they were at least less anti-Catholic. In some communities, Roman Catholics sat on school boards or served behind the desks as public school teachers. Just as the parochial schools varied from diocese to diocese, they varied from geographical region to geographical region in both number and quality. The amount of capital invested in schools varied.[4] The bishops of the "Gilded Age" were becoming increasingly concerned about the school question. The pressures on them were becoming greater with each passing year. Many Catholics found the public schools unobjectionable, and they enrolled their children in them. Others felt that they were an evil that could at best be tolerated if nothing else could be afforded. Some favored parochial schools built by direct government grants; others favored building schools and sustaining them on the basis of per pupil allotments awarded by the state. The Germans, however, were really the only solid group that seemed willing, and more than that—anxious—to protect the faith and the Old-World heritage by establishing a separate Church school system.

By 1874, eight years after the Second Plenary Council of Baltimore, many bishops were convinced that the time had come for a high-level discussion of the entire school issue as well as other problems confronting the American Church. Archbishop James Roosevelt Bayley of Baltimore persuaded Bishop Purcell of Cincinnati to host an informal conference of select members of the American hierarchy. By coincidence, just before the meeting Rome had sent off a questionnaire to the bishops of the United States on the subject of schools. It came from the Society for the Propagation of the Faith but was really instigated by a small group of American lobbyists. The leader of this cadre was James McMaster of New York, editor of the influential Catholic *Freeman's Journal*.[5] Though raised a Presbyterian, he had displayed high-church leanings that made him an unacceptable candidate for ordination to the Presbyterian ministry. He was converted to Roman Catholicism in 1845 and became a zealous member of the Church for the rest of his life. McMaster was a man of strong opinions. His pro-southern sympathies in Yankee New York earned him a brief jail sentence during the Civil War. His religious and educational views were no less strong. One of his greatest ambitions was to require every Catholic child to attend a Catholic school. With the aid of two allies in Rome, Miss Ella B. Edes, his personal agent, and Father Edmund DePauw, an American priest from New York State, McMaster drew up a memorandum and had it delivered to the offices of the Congregation of the Propaganda in February, 1874. The trio posited two questions for the study of the Congregation: Was it permissable for parents to enroll their children in a school that was in no way under the control and supervision of the Roman Catholic clergy? Was the Papal letter of July 14, 1864, addressed to the Archbishop of Fribourg concerning the necessity of Church involvement in schools applicable to the Church in the United States?[6]

The McMaster memorial was embellished by a fifteen point exposition which was chiefly the work of McMaster. In it some of the following points were raised: Catholic schools would finally determine the victory or loss of the Roman Catholic Church in the United States;[7] countless Catholics in Protestant America had already lost their faith, but this fact was dangerously masked by immigration statistics which made the Church appear to grow year after year; the American Church was not united to combat this problem because there was deep division among members of the hierarchy; the Protestant threat was real and serious; state certification requirements were required in the public schools;[8] anti-Catholic books continued to be forced upon Catholic children in the public schools as was the "Protestant Bible;" coeducation of the sexes was common practice in public schools;[9] and it was not unusual when public school teachers had to be dismissed for inappropriate conduct. McMaster concluded that almost every Catholic parish in the United States could afford a school if the parishioners set their minds to it, and therefore, all that was needed to establish a nationwide network of schools was a formal directive to that effect from each diocesan bishop. For good measure, McMaster concluded by quoting the *Syllabus of Errors* of Pope Pius IX. This McMaster Memorial remains one of the very few instances in the history of American Catholic education where an American Catholic drew largely upon papal teachings to formulate a school policy. McMaster offered no empirical proof to bolster some of his rather fantastic allegations. The propositions, considered as a whole, were a comprehensive statement of the conservative position, one that would find its widest acceptance among the Germans. Though he could only hope to have done so at the time, McMaster had laid down the rationale for the educational decrees of the Third Plenary Council of Baltimore of 1884.

McMaster's communication strongly implied that public schools in the United States, because of the teachers, curricula, and other non-Catholic factors, were very real occasions of sin. The members of the Roman Congregation were obviously struck by this presentation and by April had prepared a questionnaire designed to poll the opinion of the American hierarchy on the subject in order to gather more data upon which to base a final settlement. There were five items on the question sheet sent out by the Holy See; (1) Why do Catholics allow their children to attend non-Catholic schools? (2) How can children be reasonably kept from such schools? (3) Concerning sacramental absolution,[10] should it be withheld from parents who persist in refusing to send their children to Catholic schools? (4) Would the denial of absolution have any actual effect? (5) Might the refusal of absolution be too harmful to be practical? The individual answers submitted by each bishop to Rome have yet to be made public by Vatican authorities, but because the questionnaire was received in time for the Cincinnati meeting sponsored by Bayley and hosted by Purcell the minutes of the conference provide a measure of the general sentiments of the American hierarchy. Archbishop Bayley, it is obvious, was not an admirer of McMaster, and he seemed to have resented the questionnaire in the first place. Most of the archbishops and bishops at Cincinnati in 1874 appear to have believed that the public schools were secular but that this was hardly tantamount to their being anti-Catholic. It was generally felt that under the circumstances prevailing the establishment of parochial schools everywhere was an impossible goal. The bishops were opposed to a blanket denial of absolution because there were too many circumstances in which a parent might be truly justified in choosing a public school over a Catholic school. To formulate such a policy concerning absolution, they felt, would not only be unfair, it would be foolish public relations. The bishops were candid when they admitted that sometimes Catholic schools and Catholic school teachers were inferior to the public schools and public school teachers. The reason for this they concluded was that Catholic schools had less financial backing. It was their judgment that the most that could be done or should be done was to urge Catholic schools upon Catholic parents and this they pointed out was already accomplished by the provisions of the Second Plenary Council of 1866. The impressions of those present were put down by Bayley in a letter that was then sent out in the form of minutes of the meeting. This and individual answers returned by the bishops were collected by the Society of the Propaganda for study. There was a wide range of opinion on both sides of the issue, but most of the prelates took a more moderate stance than McMaster whom they seemed to feel was painting a blacker picture of American education than circumstances really merited. The question now was which interpretation the Holy See would accept — that of the majority of the hierarchy or that of McMaster and a sizable minority of staunchly militant conservatives.

The initial reaction of the Vatican to the incoming responses was silence. By November, 1875, the Congregation was prepared with its answer though the decision they made had been reached five months before. The formal promulgation of the rulings, however, was not made in the United States for another year, that is, on November 24, 1876. It was apparent from a cursory glance at this so-called Instruction of 1875 that the victory was for McMaster or, more accurately, the conservative wing. Rome had taken a position differing from that expressed in the Cincinnati "minutes," but this was the age of ultramontanism, and there was little outcry. The document contained eight major sections. The first related how American public schools were "most dangerous and very much opposed to Catholicity." Then followed a description of some of the ill effects that could result when "teachers are selected from every sect indiscriminately . . ." The Congregation fathers stated that the famous papal letter to the Archbishop of Fribourg was an expression of divine and natural law and was, therefore, universally applicable. Though they did not say they were doing it, they had answered one of McMaster's two questions. The fourth point was the most significant and read:

> It only remains . . . for prelates to use every means in their power to keep the flocks committed to their care from all contact with public schools. All are agreed that there is nothing so needful to this end as the establishment of Catholic schools in every place,—and schools no whit inferior to the public ones. Every effort, then, must be directed towards starting Catholic schools where they are not, and where they are, towards enlarging them and providing them with better accommodations and equipment until they have nothing to suffer as regards teachers or equipment, by comparison with public schools. And to carry out so holy and necessary a work, the aid of religious brotherhoods and of sisterhoods will be found advantageous where the bishop sees fit to introduce them. In order that the faithful may the more freely contribute the necessary expenses, the bishops themselves should not fail to impress on them, at every suitable occasion, whether by pastoral letter, sermon or private conversation, that as bishops they would be recreant to their duty if they failed to do their utmost to provide Catholic schools. This point should be especially brought to the attention of the more wealthy and influential Catholics and members of the legislature.

Point five of the Instruction was concerned with the overall wealth of the United States and seemed to imply an acceptance on the part of the Holy See of the McMaster thesis that Catholic schools feasibly could be set up throughout the country. The sixth point was a concession to the moderates as it expressed agreement with the contention that Catholics might go to non-Catholic schools if there were no proximate danger of sin though any such determination and decision were to be left to the "conscience and judgment of the bishop." The seventh statement of the Instruction described the safeguards to be provided for those Catholic children attending public schools, namely, catechetical instruction and censorship of lessons, books, and playmates. The last and final article was most contrary to the sentiments of many of the hierarchy. It authorized the withholding of absolution under certain circumstances in the following words:

> Parents who neglect to provide . . . necessary Christian training and instruction to their children, or who permit them to go to schools in which the ruin of their souls is inevitable, or finally, who send them to the public school without sufficient cause and without taking the necessary precautions to render the danger of perversion remote, and do so while there is a good and well equipped Catholic school in the place, or the parents have the means to send them elsewhere to be educated —that such parents, if obstinate, cannot be absolved, is evident from the moral teachings of the Church.

The document was received in the United States in the same way the Roman Court had received the responses of the American bishops two years earlier—by silence.[11] The Instruction produced no immediate effect on school policies. It was extremely significant, however, for two reasons: it was the first detailed papal statement on American education; and it formed the basis of the decrees on education of the Third Plenary Council of Baltimore.

The papal Instruction was issued in 1875. It did not accurately reflect the consensus of opinion of the American hierarchy. It did not put an end to the school controversy. In fact, the question became more and more heatedly debated. By 1884 many American prelates, but most importantly the Holy See, felt it was time for the convening of another plenary council of all American bishops to discuss some of the problems in the Church in the United States. The time had come to bring peace upon the Church by imposing it from without by Roman dictum. Baltimore was selected as a site for the conference. It was a good choice not only because it was the oldest diocesan seat and the traditional meeting place but also because the incumbent Archbishop of Baltimore, James Gibbons, was a sensible and moderate man. The eventual appointment of Gibbons as presiding officer came as a relief to many who feared that an Italian might be named —something that would not be received well by American non-Catholics who tended to consider Roman Catholicism as a church comprised of and run by foreigners. Much of the schemata for the

Council was fitted more to Rome's desires than to those of the American prelates. The question of aiding Italian immigrants and erecting villas for seminarians ranked high on the Vatican's outline of the tentative agenda. If it had been left entirely to the bishops of the United States, there might have been no council at all in 1884. The Third Plenary Council is another instance where the Vatican failed to understand the American milieu.

The actual sessions of the conference were held late in 1884, the last on December 7. Present at Baltimore were fourteen archbishops, sixty bishops, five visiting prelates from Canada and Japan, seven abbots, one prefect apostolic, eleven monsignors, eighteen vicars general, twenty-three superiors of religious communities, twelve seminary rectors, and ninety theologians. Two observations about the composition of the conference reflect the rather typical thinking of the Roman Catholic Church at the time: all participants were men, and they were all members of the clergy. The Baltimore meeting of 1884 is sometimes considered the most important of its kind in the history of the Church in America. It was the last plenary council to have been held, and, surprisingly enough, all of the decrees and minutes have never yet been translated from Latin.[12]

Much of the discussion at Baltimore was concerned with education, but only a part of it with parochial schools. Other educational topics were seminary training, Catholic colleges, and Catholic secondary schools. If one were to quantify the various discussions, the question of seminaries, not parochial schools, would probably be the foremost. Other issues considered were the methods of selecting bishops, the establishment of new dioceses, and tenure for pastors of parishes. A pledge of silence was extracted from every council participant, and various committees were appointed to report on topics to the whole assemblage. The school committee was comprised of Archbishop Feehan of Chicago, Bishop Spalding of Peoria, Bishop Flasch of LaCrosse, and Bishop Cosgrove of Davenport. Their final report rather closely followed the scheme prepared in Rome as did the final decrees and the pastoral letter. When the report on schools was brought to the floor, the discussion was intense, extended and frank. Debate centered around two issues: (1) the relative merits of commanding as distinct from urging parents to support parish schools; and (2) a definition of what was a genuinely Catholic school. Bishop Fitzgerald of Little Rock[13] failed in his attempt to have every decree on schools prefaced with the words "we wish and we urge," and so the decision was made to command rather than recommend strongly. But the proposition of Bishop Chatard of Indianapolis that a "Catholic school" was one so defined by the local bishop was approved by the delegates.

About one fourth of the final decrees was concerned with education. As required by canon law they were submitted to the Pope for rejection, ratification or modification. Leo XIII gave his approval on September 21, 1885 after making only a few minor changes.[14] In Decree 197, it was stated that religious indifferentism, that is, the belief that one religion is as good as another, was the "actual and necessary fruit of the public schools as conducted" in the United States. This was consonant with the McMaster thesis. Some Catholics argued that millions upon millions were falling away from the Church in the United States. It is a rather hard figure to accept when one considers that the total number of Roman Catholics in the United States did not exceed ten million souls; but the belief that vast numbers of Catholics were annually losing their faith and that the secularism of the public schools was a contributing factor to this phenomenon was of grave concern to many prelates at Baltimore and, no doubt, a powerful motive for their support of the school legislation enacted.

The most significant decree on parochial schools read:

> 199. After full consideration of these matters, we [i.e., the bishops] conclude and decree:
>
> I. That near every church a parish school, where one does not yet exist, is to be built and maintained *in perpetuum* within two years of promulgation of this council, unless the bishop should decide that because of serious difficulties a delay must be granted. IV. That all Catholic parents are bound to send their children to the parish school, unless it is evident that a sufficient training in religion is given either in their own homes, or in other Catholic schools; or when because of sufficient reasons, approved by the bishop, with all due precautions and safeguards, it is licit to send them to other schools. What constitutes a Catholic school is left to the decision of the bishop.

Other decrees contained provisions affecting the schools: Instruction in education was to be included in the curriculum of American seminaries, especially in the areas of catechetics and Bible history. Normal schools were to be founded in dioceses whenever possible to assure a supply of well-trained parish school teachers. The pastor was to visit the school often and regularly, which was generally interpreted to be at least once a week. A teaching diploma issued through the diocese was to be required of all teachers in parochial schools in the diocese, and visitation committees were to be set up in each diocese to supervise the quality of instruction within the diocese. The actual decree on school boards read that:

> Within a year from the promulgation of the Council, the bishops shall name one or more priests who are most conversant with school affairs to constitute a Diocesan Board of Examination. It shall be the office of this board to examine all teachers, whether they are religious belonging to a diocesan congregation or seculars who wish to employ themselves in teaching in the parochial schools in the future, and, if they find them worthy, to grant them a testimonial or diploma of merit. Without this, no priest may lawfully engage any teacher for his school unless they have taught before the celebration of this Council. The diploma shall be valid for five years. After this period, another and final examination will be required of teachers. Besides this board for the examination of teachers for the whole diocese, the bishops, in accordance with the diversity of place and language, shall appoint several school boards, composed of one or several priests, to examine the schools in cities and rural districts. The duty of these boards shall be to visit and examine each school in their district once or even twice a year, and to transmit to the President of the diocesan board, for the information and guidance of the bishop, an accurate account of the state of the schools.

The duties of the board were to be further elaborated by each local bishop, and its membership was to be determined by him though he could permit, if he chose to do so, the selection of a lay delegation to sit with the priests on the board. It should be noted that diocesan priests and nuns and lay persons were the only ones included in this piece of legislation; but priests and nuns that belonged to non-diocesan communities, for instance the Jesuits or Dominicans, were not included. Many, therefore, were not covered at all.

In effect the responsibility for running the schools was given to the pastors, but the real authority was retained by the bishop, and pastors were warned against excessive zeal. The bishops at Baltimore obviously hoped that the curriculum, the quality of instruction, and the number of schools would be such that parents would have no valid reasons to withhold their patronage from Catholic parochial schools.

Pastors who ignored the decrees of the Council could be removed from office, and the bishops were to apply "pressure" in those parishes where the parishioners failed to support the rector in his efforts to build and maintain schools. The pastor was to have the final rights as regarded the hiring and firing of teachers.

The Pastoral Letter of 1884 issued at the conclusion of the Council had more than the usual amount of significance because the decrees and minutes of the proceedings had not been made available in English and because a promise of secrecy had been made by all participants. Archbishop Corrigan of New York chaired the committee that drafted the text of the document. "Education," it read, "in order to foster civilization must foster religion. It does not lie within the province of the State to teach religion." Parents, therefore, "simply follow their conscience by sending their children to denominational schools, where religion can have its place and influence." The bishops stated that they had two goals concerning Catholic schools: to increase their number and to perfect them. "We must multiply them," they said, "till every Catholic child in the land shall have within his reach the means of education. . . . No parish is complete till it has schools adequate to the needs of its children. . . ." In a very practical vein the bishops noted that parish debts should be removed as soon as possible to put schools on firm financial footing and also that there was no valid excuse for a parish school to be inferior to any other kind of school. Parents were warned by the bishops not to take their children out of school prematurely. The bishops emphasized the value of good books and periodicals and underscored the value of American history as part of the Catholic school curriculum as Catholic children ought not to become "partisans but patriots." All things considered, the Pastoral Letter of 1884 was a significant statement on Catholic education in the United States.

What did Baltimore III actually accomplish as far as the school issue was concerned? Certainly the official tone of the American hierarchy had changed. The bishops had gone from exhortations to the effect that the schools were desirable and that it was best if parents patronized them to a direct command that schools be built and used. But was the command obeyed? Would such a change of emphasis have been required if the great majority of Catholics was indeed convinced that parochial schools were necessary and advantageous? Was the growth in the number of Catholic schools a result of the Baltimore decrees and the Pastoral Letter of 1884 or was it for the same reasons that brought about the decrees and the letter that the schools were built?[15] Is it possibly an example of the *post hoc propter ergo hoc* fallacy to say that because the number of Catholic schools increased after 1884, it did so because of the Baltimore mandate? Actually the Council really just decreed that which was already happening. It certainly did not start the school question, and it did not settle it. There were approximately 2,500 parochial schools in the United States at the time of the Council. An examination of the numbers of parish schools over a ninety-five year period starting in 1875 reveals no sustained and consistent growth pattern. The ten year period preceding the Council witnessed the construction of approximately eleven hundred schools; the ten year period following the Council, twelve hundred. Inasmuch as the overall number of Catholics in the population rose by well over one million from 1875 to 1895, no significance can be attributed to the slight difference between the pre-Council and post-Council growth rates. Many areas were slow to implement the decrees. As before, some were more ready to build schools than others. The Baltimore Council did put the stamp of approval on the developing network of schools. It seemed to have been what the Vatican wanted. Whether the American Church fathers fully appreciated it or not, it was an official commitment to tie down a large proportion of the capital of the Church to a specific channel and limit work as a result in many other areas. By 1963, seventy-nine years later, an estimated five billion dollars had been invested with an additional annual operating cost of 850 million dollars—a fortune made even more impressive when one considers the socioeconomic origins of American Catholicity.[16]

Some see Baltimore III as a logical culmination of a long series of educational decrees of the American hierarchy. This is correct only if one views the shift from urging and exhorting to requiring and commanding as a logical and natural progression. As strong a case can be made that the decrees of Baltimore II of 1866 marked the real culmination. The pronouncements made by the bishops at the Plenary Council of that year were really a synthesis and restatement of earlier decisions made over a period spanning approximately seventy-four years. The 1884 statements reveal a movement to a more hard-line attitude.

Yet the Church in the 1880's was certainly no more beleaguered than it had been in the 1840's, 1850's, or 1860's. There were more Catholics than ever before, comprising an ever larger part of the total national population. The public schools were probably less anti-Catholic than they had been in the earlier period. So why the stronger position? The answer is already manifest: the Baltimore Council of 1884 took a stronger position on education because of papal pressures and because of the growing influence of the German-conservative elements. Rather than searching for the origins of the decrees of 1884 in those of the various preceding councils of Baltimore, one should study the decrees of the councils held in selected centers of conservative strength, most especially in the pronouncements of the Province of Cincinnati, one of the great sees in the German triangle. The decrees of the Second Provincial Council of Cincinnati of 1858 read in part:

> It is the judgment of the Fathers that all pastors of souls are bound, under pain of mortal sin, to provide a Catholic school in every parish or congregation subject to them, where this can be done; and in order that each Ordinary may know what are the parishes in which this obligation exists, they decree that the Tridentine Law, s. XXII, c. IX, is to be practically enforced, by which rectors of churches are required each year to render an exact account to their Ordinaries of all revenues accruing to their churches in any way, which they therefore strictly enjoin as to be observed by aforesaid rectors.[17]

Even though this decree was handed down eight years before the Second Plenary Council of 1866, the national hierarchy took a decidedly more moderate position, indicating, perhaps, their unwillingness to go further without prodding.

The effect of the decrees of 1884 on Catholic education has been exaggerated. The schools built in the immediately ensuing years would probably have been built anyway. A strong argument for schools could have been drawn before the Council from earlier decrees and from canon law. Even after 1884 the debate on the school question waged on more intensely within the Church.

The basic positions being stated, Catholic leaders seemed to reflect either the liberal or the conservative viewpoint. The liberals were less intent in their support of a parochial school system than were the conservatives. In the forefront of liberal ranks were John Ireland, Archbishop of St. Paul, John Lancaster Spalding, Bishop of Peoria,[18] and Bishop John Keane, longtime Rector of the Catholic University of America in Washington, D. C. The sentiments of James Cardinal Gibbons, Archbishop of Baltimore, were also with this group. These liberals might be labelled the "Irish school." The older, that is, more "Americanized" groups including the Irish, tended to side with this faction. They felt that the Church was best served by supporting every kind of educational enterprise, including the public schools. They shared the common American faith in the power of education and believed that education would indeed make a man a better citizen. To a degree they shared a little of the Rousseauian optimism regarding the perfectibility of man and the goodness of human nature, and they advocated a good, practical education for women. Not altogether unfavorably disposed to some of the new educational reforms, some of the liberals even praised such innovators as Froebel and envisioned a wider scope for education than mere doctrinal inculcation. If this group is to be labelled the "Irish school," it must be noted that this was second-generation Irish. Much of the militancy of the era of Bishop John Hughes was gone. Yet the liberals were not so staid as the Catholics of the era of Archbishop John Carroll. Militancy seemed to have decreased somewhat with "Americanization." Many in this camp, no doubt, felt intimidated by the Instruction of 1875 and the Baltimore mandates of 1884.

Opposing them was the conservative wing of the American Church which might be accurately called the "German school." The German immigrants provided the muscle power to this group even though many of its leaders were by no means German. It is difficult to assess the precise numbers in the opposing camps. Most Catholics were oblivious to the raging storm. The Germans were destined to win out because their more conservative viewpoint was more consonant with that of the Church Universal. It is probably correct to say that Cardinal Gibbons, while personally sharing the liberal philosophy, was astute enough to comprehend the futility of bucking the system and of trying to implement a policy that smacked of indifferentism and statism in the eyes of a papacy buoyed by ultramontanism against an oncoming tide of nationalism, anticlericalism, secularism, and materialism in late nineteenth-century Europe. The conservative faction likewise contained some very remarkable personalities in its ranks. These included, of course, James McMaster and his silent partner,

Ella Edes. It also included Bernard McQuaid, Bishop of Rochester in New York,[19] William Corrigan, a protégé of McQuaid's and Archbishop of New York, and the bishops of Wisconsin. Unlike their liberal confreres, these men had less faith in the benefits of formal education. Many doubted that any amount of schooling would really eliminate anti-Catholic prejudice. The majority of them felt that the woman's place was in the home and hence that there was no need for her to have a fancy education. Conservatives had quite understandably been more satisfied with the educational decrees of Baltimore III than had been the liberals. Like the liberals, however, they felt that the Catholic schools were entitled to public funds, but unlike the liberals their demands for state aid were more uncompromising, more militant, and no doubt more irksome to the non-Catholic majority.

Probably the most influential American Church figure of the era was John Ireland of Saint Paul, Minnesota.[20] Though Archbishop Gibbons was better known he did not seem to have left such a mark upon the times. Gibbons was the picture of sacerdotal splendor, tall, slim, and handsome in his prelate's robes. He looked type-cast for the role he played. Gibbons was, in many ways, the Fulton Sheen of his age, the name that the man on the street would give when asked to name an important Roman Catholic bishop. But Ireland seems to have dominated the period. No one had lukewarm feelings about him. A revealing nickname of Ireland's was "the consecrated blizzard of the Northwest." One of the German conservatives, however, preferred the variant "the Anti-Christ of the North." Ireland was not the scholar of Spalding's caliber, nor was he a diplomat like Gibbons, but he was a charismatic leader. His personality bore many of the traits of Theodore Roosevelt's, and his ideas, of Rooseveltian Progressivism. Indeed the liberal and conservative factions can be defined in terms of Bishop Ireland. He was, of course, a liberal, and influenced in his ideas on education by Dr. Thomas Bocquillon, a professor at Catholic University in Washington, D. C.

In 1890 he accepted an invitation to address the annual convention of the National Education Association which was then being held in Saint Paul, Minnesota. The speech caused nothing short of a sensation. Ireland said he favored public schools and parish schools too under certain circumstances. He said he hoped that the day would come when there would no longer be a need for parochial schools to exist at all. Ireland went on record as favoring compulsory attendance at public schools or other accredited institutions. As for aid to education, said Ireland, "Money paid in school tax is the money of the State, and is to be disbursed only for the specific purposes for which it was collected. The free school of America!" he went on with a dramatic flourish, "withered be the hand raised in sign of its destruction!" He concluded that the ideal would be to have "Christian state schools," and he suggested a shared time formula which he was to implement personally a year later.

Reports of the address were carried in newspapers across the country. The "Germans" were almost apoplectic. Many, like Bishop McQuaid, felt Ireland was proposing nothing short of a total abandonment of the parochial school system and an abrogation of the Baltimore decrees. Some non-Catholics criticized the address as a crafty Catholic plan to seize control of the public schools. Ireland, on the other hand, felt that he was being misinterpreted and that parts of his address were being taken out of context and being exploded into great issues. Gibbons privately favored Ireland's ideas, but when pressed for an opinion on the matter by Pope Leo, he asked Ireland to clarify his position in writing. Ireland responded that it had been his intention to use the national audience offered by the NEA convention to dispel the notion that Catholics were opposed to education in general, to the State's establishing and maintaining schools, and to compulsory attendance laws. "America," he wrote to Cardinal Gibbons:

> is not a 'Protestant State,' and if Catholics pay school taxes they should receive benefit from them. The burden upon our Catholics to maintain parish schools up to the required standard for all the children of the Church is almost unbearable. There is danger that never shall we have schools for all Catholic children, or that Catholics will grow tired of contributing. At present nearly half of the Catholic children of America do not attend parish-schools. The true solution, in my judgment, is to make the State-School satisfactory to Catholic consciences, and to use it. Can this be done? Let us try. If it cannot be done, let us do our best with our parish-schools.

Ireland had already caused hard feelings in Wisconsin by his statements regarding the Bennet law which required that English be taught at least sixteen weeks out of every school year in every school in the state. The German bishops of Wisconsin protested against the law on the grounds that it was undue interference, but Ireland gratuitously went on public record as favoring it.

In August, 1891, Archbishop Ireland entered into a plan with the school boards of Stillwater and Faribault, Minnesota. This program was an implementation of his earlier shared-time proposal to the NEA meeting in Saint Paul. The program was hardly revolutionary as it was then being used or had been tried in a similar form in Boston, Savannah, Hartford, Newark, Cleveland, Poughkeepsie, Missouri, and Pennsylvania. The parochial school building was to be leased to the public school board for a nominal fee. Nuns or Catholic teachers approved by the regular school board were to staff the school. Religious instruction was to be given but after regular school hours. Ireland found that he had few supporters on this issue. Even Bishop John Spalding of Peoria disapproved of the program. Conservatives were shocked by it even though other experiments in shared time had taken place within conservative bailiwicks. Faribault, however, was in the Province of Saint Paul, and with a man like Ireland in charge many conservatives feared that such an expedient as shared time might become standard practice instead of an extraordinary exception. The American Protective Association, which was really nothing more than the nativist response to the post-Civil War wave of immigration, opposed the plan on the grounds that it was a violation of the principle of separation of Church and State. In April, 1892, the Vatican gave its tacit approval of Ireland's program when it said it could be tolerated, that is, *"tolerari potest,"* but at the same time it stated that the Baltimore decrees of 1884 were still very much in effect. The Vatican's phrasing was vague. It gave Ireland the endorsement he had wanted but certainly in less strong terms than he had hoped. It also left some hope for conservatives who interpreted the pontifical statement as one of disapproval. Ironically, Ireland's program collapsed shortly thereafter because of political conditions in Minnesota.

The idea of shared time did not die with the Faribault and Stillwater programs, however, and has been raised many times since then. Contemporary advocates of such plans seem to overlook a more recent statement on the subject issued by the Vatican in 1929. Pope Pius XI voiced disapproval when he wrote in his encyclical letter on education:

> the so-called 'neutral' or 'lay' school from which religion is excluded is contrary to the fundamental principles of education. Such a school

The Era Of The Germans

moreover cannot exist in practice; it is bound to become irreligious ... The frequenting of non-Catholic schools, whether neutral or mixed, those namely which are open to Catholics and non-Catholics alike, is forbidden for Catholic children, and can at most be tolerated, on the approval of the Ordinary alone, under determined conditions. Neither can Catholics admit that other type of mixed school (least of all the so-called 'ecole unique' obligatory to all), in which the students are provided with separate religious instruction, but receive other lessons in common with non-Catholic pupils from non-Catholic teachers.

Catholic opinion, then, during the nineteen-twenties and thirties seemed to have changed to one of opposition to shared-time and released-time programs. One respected Catholic authority on education at the time of the encyclical wrote that "certainly it must be admitted that Archbishop Ireland's plan was a dangerous compromise in fact, although certainly not in the intent of the eminent prelate."[21] One of the chief concerns of opponents to such plans is the resulting heterogeneity of the student body, that is, non-Catholics being educated with Catholics.

The Supreme Court of the United States in 1948 declared in the McCollum Case, in an 8 to 1 decision, that shared time was unconstitutional, that is, school children may not receive religious instruction during school hours on public school property even though it is being given by privately employed teachers. Released time, that is, permitting early dismissal of children from school to receive religious instruction at locations other than public school property has been upheld by the Supreme Court in the Zorach Case of 1952. Ireland's program differed slightly from each of these. Religious instruction was to be given in the same building but after school hours when, according to the arrangements with the school board, the property was technically back in the hands of the Church. Futhermore, religious instruction was to be provided by the same teachers though the costs for these after-school services were to be met from parish funds. How today's courts would decide on Ireland's program is a moot point but an interesting one for speculation since one hears it advanced now and again as a possible solution to the financial crisis in the Catholic schools. Forms of released-time arrangements are now being attempted in Chicago and elsewhere.

Ireland delivered his NEA address late in 1890 and negotiated the Stillwater and Faribault plans in August, 1891. In May, 1892 Leo gave his permission for the scheme; but in the summer he sent Archbishop Francis Satolli to the United States as his personal representative. One of his missions was to determine the degree to which the Baltimore decrees were being implemented. It was the contention of Archbishop Spalding that the Faribault episode gave the Vatican a pretext for setting up a permanent Apostolic Delegation in the United States, something it had long wanted to do anyway. This would give the Holy Father a first hand source of information. By November of that year the papal ablegate[22] was ready with his reports and recommendations. His dispatch to the Vatican appeared to be a vindication of Ireland's position. He approved of the public schools with reservations and forbade the withholding of the sacraments from parents who refused to send their children to parochial schools. The following fourteen points were embodied in Satolli's statement on schools: (1) Catholic schools were to be made the equals in quality of public schools; (2) Catholics could go to public schools if this would not incur a proximate danger of moral perversion; (3) only qualified persons could be employed as Catholic school teachers; (4) normal schools were to be set up for the training of Catholic teachers whenever possible; (5) children and parents were not to be cut off from the sacraments for withholding support from Catholic schools; (6) there was nothing intrinsically wrong when Catholic children learned nonreligious subjects in public schools; (7) public schools were to be considered desirable only when devoid of elements that are opposed to Christianity and morality; (8) Catholic children may attend public schools if the dangers described in the Baltimore documents have been obviated; (9) the final decision to build schools or not to build schools rests solely with the bishop; (10) parents are not be condemned for sending their children to good private schools instead of parish schools; (11) programs such as that at Faribault can be tolerated;[23] (12) when possible the following programs should be set up for children in public schools: shared time or released time or catechism classes; (13) ideally, Catholic school teachers should hold state teaching certificates as well as diocesan diplomas; (14) Catholics should pursue programs of studies for graduate degrees. This document issued by Archbishop Satolli was to be only a temporary victory for the liberals, however, even though Leo defended his ablegate from the wrath of the conservatives. Many of them would have endorsed Bishop McQuaid's analysis that "Mgr [Monsignor] Satolli's propositions concede[d] too much." On May 31 the Pope stated that all Baltimore decrees were definitely in effect as originally promulgated and that any concession that had been made by Satolli or implied by him in his propositions was nugatory. The ablegate remained in the United States but by 1895 had definitely shifted to the German position. The Vatican, as would become more evident in the next few years, was also leaning more toward the conservative side if it had indeed ever had a momentary attack of liberalism. The German-conservative position was wholly in consonance with the ultramontanism embraced by the Vatican.

The dissension in the Church over the school question was only one facet of a much larger controversy raging over the entire issue of "Americanism." The conservatives were distrustful of all forms of republican government, which they lumped together as "Americanist," and considered them by their very nature opposed to religion. They felt that the liberals were so anxious to accommodate themselves to the new age that they were willing to compromise the fundamentals of traditional Catholicism. It was necessary, argued the conservatives, to have special schools to protect the religious needs of the child. The "Americanists" or liberals, on the other hand, felt that a democratic government was the most realistic approach to modern pluralism and that pragmatism (not in the purely Deweyan sense) was a workable way to treat cultural problems.

Despite its name much of the impetus behind "Americanism" was European.[24] The average American Catholic was almost completely unaware of the controversy. Unfortunately, the school issue, along with several others, became quite confused with certain doctrinal matters that were too naturalistic for the mainstream of orthodox Catholic beliefs, and Pope Leo XIII condemned the "Americanist heresy" in an encyclical letter entitled *Testem Benevolentiae* in 1899. An excellent précis of the pontifical pronouncement appeared in the March 4, 1899 issue of the *San Francisco Monitor*:

> ... It was a plain and simple letter dealing principally with the matters of doctrine which nobody ever had the least intention of disputing. The questions of discipline are not of general importance and concern only a few persons in America ...
> ... Every people have their own characteristics, every nation its own laws and customs. The American people are Americans, not German, or French, or Anglo-Saxon or Irish. The genius of a people will neces-

sarily show itself in religion as well as political affairs. The Church in France and Italy and Ireland while it is the same church essentially is yet not altogether the same. But the difference is not a matter of faith or morals, and arises from the different dispositions and traditions and customs of the different races. That difference shows itself distinctly among the Catholic people of foreign birth in this country and this is the cause of the whole difficulty. To erase this difference as far as possible and to make the Catholics in America one homogeneous body in touch with the institutions of the country and partaking of the genius of the American people—this is the "Americanism" that Archbishop Ireland and his friends stand for. This the Pope has not condemned and never will condemn, because to do so would be an important attempt to stop the natural progress of things which cannot be effected. It is a pity that such a question as "Americanism" should ever have been raised.[25]

The papal letter was unfortunate. It ended discussion, but it failed to solve the underlying problems. It was yet another instance of a lack of understanding on the part of the Vatican of the American milieu. The Pope and his advisors failed to distinguish adequately between American and French republicanism. They tended to believe too many of the things they were told by the conservatives. In America no one really held any of the false theological doctrines, and many were seriously offended by the papal missive. By raising the charge of heresy the Vatican had in effect put a damper on many forms of speculative discussion. This outcome was magnified by the *Syllabus* of Pope Pius X in 1907 in which he condemned sixty-five propositions of "Modernism" which was a sort of omnibus heresy which held such things as the denial of the divinity of Christ, the divine inspiration of the Bible, and the objective validity of religion. More and more the bishops turned away from the speculative issues and concentrated instead almost exclusively on brick-and-mortar problems. This is not to imply that U.S. bishops were deeply embroiled in theological controversies. As a rule, the rapid growth rate of the Church had denied them this luxury. The fact that the Church in America was divided into dissenting factors remained basically unchanged until World War I.

During the first decade of the twentieth century, the situation became considerably calmer. The bishops said less and settled down to the business of erecting schools and churches. By 1910 the Catholic Church had "publicly committed itself to the parochial school as the only solution to the educational problem." There were twice as many Roman Catholics in the country as there had been in 1880 and about twice as many schools with three times the enrollment. It was no longer a choice between public school, no school, or expensive private academy; the parochial school was a viable alternative for the majority of Catholic parents. By the turn of the century, too, the socioeconomic status of the typical Catholic was improving. Certainly he was not yet the equal of his aristocratic Maryland-English predecessor, but, then, he was better off than the recently arrived immigrant of a generation earlier. This change began to be reflected in the Catholic schools. In the older communities of Catholic settlement, the schools were not quite so defensive, nor were they so almost exclusively concerned with preserving the ethnic subculture. This subtle change was somewhat mitigated by the newer but comparatively smaller waves of immigration of southern and eastern Europeans such as the Italians, Hungarians, Poles, and Slavs.

Since the 1830's and 1840's two contradictory forces have been at work within the Catholic school system: one has been the pressure to preserve the culture and the language of the foreign immigrant group; the other has been the drive for assimilation of that group into the mainstream of American culture. The new arrivals have traditionally stressed the former; and the older groups, the latter. Hence the old-English minority battled with the Irish before the Civil War; the Irish, with the Germans during the "Gilded Age;" and, to a lesser extent, the northern and western Europeans, with the southern and eastern Europeans in the first decades of this century. Some evidence of these same forces may be seen in operation today in predominantly Puerto Rican parishes. These factors act as motives for establishing and maintaining parochial schools, and both of them are now at their lowest general level since before the 1830's. There are very few new Catholics coming into the United States today as immigrants, and for the most part Catholics have been assimilated into the culture. The period when the parochial school system really got underway was during the time of greatest interaction between these twin drives to preserve the culture and to be assimilated, that is, during the period of the Americanist conflict of the 1880's and 1890's. This may present a key to understanding the present Catholic school crisis. The problems of the schools are possibly at their greatest level, and yet

Catholics are in a better position to support these schools financially than ever before in the history of American Catholicism. The twin motives are no longer very strong—one has been achieved and the other has been largely removed by time.

By the end of the nineteenth century one could speak with some degree of accuracy about a Catholic school "system." Long before Baltimore III the movement to organize parish schools into diocesan networks had begun. Bishop Neumann of Philadelphia had taken pioneering steps along these lines in 1852 by setting up a Central Board of Education comprised of pastors and two laymen from each parish. In 1879 Bishop Dwenger of Fort Wayne, Indiana, brought all of the parish schools in his diocese under his more immediate control by creating a school board of eleven members and a secretary, all of whom were priests. This board was more powerful than the Philadelphia body but less powerful than its public school board counterpart. The bishop really acted as the superintendent of schools, and the pastors, as deputy superintendents. The Catholic school board was appointed by the bishop-superintendent whereas the public school board usually chose its own chief school executive. In 1882, just two years before Baltimore III, the bishops of the Province of Cincinnati adopted the Fort Wayne model for all schools within the dioceses of the Province. The fathers at Baltimore III decreed that each diocese in the United States was to have a diocesan school board with local boards after the pattern of Cincinnati, providing yet another example of the German influence at the 1884 meeting. By the end of the century, Cleveland, LaCrosse, Detroit, Louisville, Hartford, Belleville, Duluth, and Wichita had set up boards in compliance with the decrees—eight dioceses within fifteen years, a small percentage of the national total, and most of them in the Middle West. This too points to the fact that the real influence of the Third Plenary Council on Catholic parochial school development has been exaggerated. It is quite possible that these dioceses would have organized their schools without any prodding. Some dioceses were also creating the office of school superintendent and filling it with priests. These school superintendents very often were not professional educators or school administrators by training, and they were not really very independent of the local bishop. They were less powerful than their public school counterparts. There were no William Torrey Harrises or Ella

Flagg Youngs.²⁶ About the same time there developed the position of "community inspector"—a religious with authority to inspect all the schools of a given order in a given diocese. Non-diocesan orders did not come under the direct control of the diocesan authorities, but rather of the Congregation of Religious in Rome.

The National Catholic Education Association (NCEA) was established in 1904, and it continues to seek to unite Catholic educators and promote the general interests of Catholic education throughout the United States. It is an attempt to provide a means of articulation between the various diocesan and regional units of the American parochial school system. By 1969, it had about fifteen thousand members, sponsored its sixty-sixth annual meeting to treat of various problems confronting Catholic educators at all levels, and continued to act as a lobby in Washington for the Catholic schools. The quarterly bulletin of the Association and the published reports of its proceedings are a significant source for the study of recent Catholic educational history. Much of the success of the NCEA can be attributed to its executive secretaries, George Johnson, Frederick Hochwalt, and the incumbent C. Albert Koob. After a recent revamping of the administrative structure of the NCEA, Father Koob's title was changed to President.

Four men occupied the papal throne between the American Civil War and the end of World War I: Pius IX, Leo XIII, Pius X, and Benedict XV. All were Italians, and all were rather strong leaders. During the reign of Pius IX the Vatican lost its control over the Papal States to the forces of Italian nationalism, but the influence of the papacy in the spiritual domain did not seem diminished. At the First Vatican Council held in Rome in 1870, the fathers of the Church gave their vote of approval to an official declaration of the infallibility of the pope when he speaks formally on matters of faith and morals. Though it was not by any means a new idea in the Church, it was not without its opponents. Many prelates were opposed to the declaration, and many had reservations that fell somewhere between outright opposition and the staunch support of the measure accorded by the ultramontanists. Though the opponents to the measure were in a minority, their strength in 1870 has too often been minimized. Many American bishops disapproved of the declaration, but all eventually submitted to it after its enactment at the ecumenical council.

The trend in the Roman Church by 1860 was toward an increased centralization and a more intense devotionalism. The 1870 declaration helped clarify the position of the pope in the structure of the Church. The number of encyclicals, constitutions, decrees, instructions, and allocutions from the throne multiplied. The aura of infallibility clung to most papal statements despite the fact that it was intended to apply only to official declarations on important matters of faith and to grave religious issues. John Cardinal Newman remarked that the intellectual life in the Church had come to consist largely of analysing papal teachings. The Roman mode of worship gained ever wider acceptance in the liturgy, in church music, and in religious dress—often at the expense of local customs. The conservatives carried the day, but not without some opposition. The papal influence was felt more and more in the Church after 1860 and would continue to be an important factor until long after the period under consideration.

Pope Pius IX was a saintly man, and his term of office, spanning more than thirty years, was one of the longest and most depressing in the history of the papacy. It was during his reign that the Vatican "lost" the Papal States which had been a part of its legacy from the time of Pepin in the eighth century. It was Pius IX who presided over the stormy sessions of Vatican I. More important for American Catholic education, it was Pius who issued the famous Instruction of 1875 that later became the basis of the educational decrees of Baltimore III. This Instruction was the first major pontifical statement on education expressly addressed to American Catholics. It is noteworthy that the Instruction was issued under the seal of Pope Pius IX but that the Baltimore decrees of 1884 received the stamp of approval of Pope Leo XIII who succeeded him in 1878. There was no discernible difference between the policies of Leo and Pius on the question of American parochial schools. This is not surprising. Leo and Pius shared the same general outlook on many things. It had been Leo years before who had first suggested the idea of the *Syllabus of Errors* to Pius IX. Leo was then Vincent Cardinal Pecci.

Leo had been a papal diplomat before becoming Pope. He was highly intelligent and very well educated. In addition he was a fine administrator and was generally quite popular in Catholic circles. In America he was well liked by both liberals and conservatives. During

The Era Of The Germans

his pontificate of twenty-five years, he issued an unprecedented number of pronouncements, letters and other written teachings. Many of these were quite abstract and dealt in general principles. Many were quite progressive for their time though they appear rather timid by today's standards. The *Rerum Novarum* of 1891 dealing with social justice and the working man was, possibly, his finest work. It was not directly concerned with education. Other major Leonine encyclicals are noteworthy because they are revealing of the prevailing attitudes in the Church at that time. For instance, in one encyclical Leo stated that it was no less than "a public crime" for the State to carry on as if there were no God and show no care for religion.[27] It is wrong, too, he wrote, for the State "to hold in equal favor different kinds of religion. . . ." In another letter Leo wrote that the "liberty of worship" is opposed to the virtue of religion and the profession of a single religion is necessary in the State.[28] In a rare letter directed to the situation in the United States, Leo stated that "the unbridled liberty of thought and of the press . . . is the root and fountain-head of immoral opinions. Religion having been in the majority of cases exiled from [the American public?] schools, criminal men are boldly laboring to extinguish by deceits of false wisdom, the Christian faith in the souls of adolescents, and to enkindle impiety."[29]

Other writings of the Pope were more directly concerned with education. During the first years of his pontificate he seemed especially concerned with the exclusion of the Church from the public schools in Rome. Leo opposed the creation of so-called "neutral-schools," that is, those from which all religion was excluded. Leo also publicly went on record as upholding the right of every bishop to superintend all areas of education within the boundaries of his diocese. In America this would presumably include the public school which, of course, could be nothing but a declaration on paper as no state would recognize the legal right of Catholic bishops to supervise any of the activities going on in state schools. One of Pope Leo's more curious and understandably human remarks was that it was lamentable that some historians were teaching that the civil authority of the Pope had been bad for Italy. In the same year that the American bishops met at Baltimore, Leo stated that it was his belief that Freemasons had had much to do with the secularization of schools.

As has already been noted, the Baltimore declarations received pontifical approval in 1885, and Leo consistently upheld these enactments throughout his reign. He said that they were "to be steadfastly observed" in a letter to Cardinal Gibbons and the American hierarchy in 1893. He praised the decrees in an encyclical in 1895, and he frequently lauded those who supported the building of private Catholic schools as alternatives to secular public instruction. Another of the more curious of Leo's letters on the topic of education was that addressed to the bishops of the Province of New York in 1892. In it the Pope urged the creation of Catholic schools, an interesting comment inasmuch as it was made eight years after Baltimore III. Were the Catholics of New York remiss in their duty thereby meriting a "nudge" from the Pontiff? Certainly McQuaid and Corrigan needed no encouragement. "We think that nobody there [in New York]," continued the Holy Father, "will tolerate an obligation on the part of Catholic parents to protect and promote primary and secondary schools which they cannot make use of to educate their own children." This was nothing other than an early variation of the argument of "double taxation," that is, Catholic parents are under an especially difficult obligation: they must pay public school taxes because of the law, but because of their consciences which deem these schools unacceptable, they must contribute to the support of separate Catholic schools what is tantamount to a second tax.

Leo declared that Catholics ought not to patronize schools where Catholics and non-Catholics were educated together. "Let nobody easily persuade himself," he went on, "that piety can be separated from instruction with impunity. Religion must not be taught to youth only during certain hours, but the entire system of education must be permeated with a sense of Christian piety." On another occasion, Leo wrote, "We must avoid at all costs those unfortunate schools where religious beliefs are indifferently admitted with equal treatment, as if, in the things that regard God and divine affairs, it matters little to have or not to have the right doctrines or to embrace truth or error. . . . All such schools have been condemned by the Church. . . ."

Leo's influence on the future of the Church was significant. As regards the "Catholic philosophy of education,"[30] he was a traditionalist. He said more than any previous pontiff on the subject, but he really said nothing that had not been said before by other popes. Because he tended to put his thoughts into writing and because he wrote often and well, succeeding popes drew much from the Leonine letters. An examination of the documentation of the more significant papal teachings of the next half century reveals the extent of the indebtedness of the successors of Pope Leo in this regard.

Joseph Sarto, Patriarch of Venice, succeeded Leo as Pope in 1903 and took the name of Pius X. He was of an entirely different cut from that of Leo: Leo had been a diplomat, Pius, a pastor; Leo was of high birth, Pius, of more humble origins. If Leo was a traditionalist, Pius was a reactionary. He was not so prolific a writer as was Leo. His encyclical *Pascendi Dominici Gregis* of 1907 which condemned "Modernism" also recommended a number of measures designed to check the spread of the heresy: revival of Thomistic studies, reform of seminary curricula, greater care in the selection of seminary faculty, institutions of committees of vigilance, and stricter censorship of clerical publications. A year later, the Holy Father removed the Catholic Church in the United States from the status of a mission country by withdrawing it from the jurisdiction of the Congregation for the Propagation of the Faith. A rather unusual letter on education was addressed by the Pope to the Christian Brothers. In it he stated that:

> We have heard that an opinion is being diffused which claims that for you the education of children should take first place and the religious profession second place ... We absolutely do not want to find this opinion gaining even the slightest credit in your Institute or in other religious institutes, which, like yours, have as their end the education of youth ... Let it be very clear then that in many things the religious life stands above the lay life, and that, if you are gravely bound to your neighbor by the duty to teach, much more serious are the obligations that bind you to God.

This is an interesting comment in light of contemporary writings on the role of the laity in the modern Church. Pius shared some of his predecessors' misgivings about public schools. "The necessity of . . . Christian instruction," he wrote, "seems to have increased, both because of the progress of the times and of modern ways, and as a result of those public schools, where it is considered amusing to deride everything holy."

Pope Pius X died on the eve of World War I and was succeeded by Giacomo Della Chiesa who became Benedict XV. The new Pope shared the basic philosophy of his immediate predecessors. He wholeheartedly endorsed the stand of Pius X on Modernism. In one of his few statements on education he praised the Church in the United States for its efforts on behalf of parochial schools. In America, he told the bishops, "You will have no Christians other than those instructed and educated by you." Pope Benedict died in 1922 and was followed on the throne by Pope Pius XI.

Catholic education was also affected by the promulgation of a new code of canon law in 1918. The regulations were really only an updated form of the existing laws on the Church's statute books but in a more modern and usable form. The essential provisions of the Instruction of 1875 and of the Baltimore decrees of 1884 were restated. The new *Codex* gave the clergy a sort of code-of-canon-law complex. The provisions of the *Codex* hung like the sword of Damocles over the heads of priests and bishops to be shaken loose at the merest hint of violation of the letter of the law. The recodification was begun by Pius X and was continued and completed by Benedict XV.

Of the papal statements on education issued between 1860 and 1920, the Instruction of 1875 appears to have been the most significant. The general body of writings of Pope Leo XIII is larger and seemingly more significant than those issued by Pius IX, Pius X, or Benedict XV.

* * *

The fifty-year period of American Catholic history spanning the years 1870 to 1920 might be viewed as an epoch and labeled the "Era of the Germans" just as the periods before 1870 might be called the "Era of the Irish" and the "Era of the English." The fifty-year period in question was marked by an immense wave of immigration, but unlike those newcomers of previous periods, these were largely of non-English-speaking origins. The largest bloc was comprised of Germans who tended to settle in the Middle West. Just as the Irish had attempted to wrest control of the machinery of the Church from the older English-Catholic core, these contended with the "Americanized" Irish. The Irish tended to look down upon the foreigner with disdain very much as they themselves had been viewed earlier by the English Catholics. The Irish had won their "battle" with the older core by sheer force of numbers. The Germans were to win by capturing the ear of the Vatican.

The Era Of The Germans

By this time the public schools were generally accepted as part and parcel of the American heritage. While not so anti-Catholic as they had originally been, they were hardly secular, but rather nondenominational Protestant in cast. The idea that some sort of formal schooling was desirable was generally accepted by American Catholics, but there was deep division over the necessity of building Catholic parochial schools as an alternative to public school education throughout the entire country. The older Catholic groups were inclined for a variety of reasons to say "not necessary"—the newcomers, "absolutely essential." The great center of the parochial school movement came to rest in the Middle West, especially in the Province of Cincinnati and in the state of Wisconsin.

The Vatican became increasingly concerned about the school issue. Reports coming to Rome were conflicting. Eventually the interpretation of the newcomers, that is, of the German-conservative faction, to the effect that the public schools presented a grave threat to American Catholicity was accepted by the Vatican. Orders were issued to build schools, but they had little real effect. The Vatican then instigated a national meeting of the hierarchy which dittoed the earlier mandates of the Holy See. Still the controversy was not settled but raged on for several years. Various papal writings underscored the school decrees. The official tone had changed from that of the era before 1870. Schools were no longer merely encouraged; they were made mandatory. The pontifical writings of the period on education were increasingly numerous, and occasionally they were addressed to the Church in America and made available in English. Still they seemed more relevant to the European milieu than to that of the United States.

Nevertheless, by the second decade of the present century, the American Catholic parochial school system was well on its way to becoming an important and sizable facet of American education. The commitment had officially been made to establish a network of Catholic schools across the country. There were several reasons for the success of the parochial school movement, but the major official documents, namely, the Instruction of 1875, the decrees of the Third Plenary Council of Baltimore of 1884, and the *Codex* of 1918, do not seem to have been as significant as other factors. Probably the most important of these was the improving socioeconomic condition of the typical Catholic—he could more comfortably afford private schools. Other factors were the desire to preserve ethnic integrity and to retain denominational purity. Many thought that the Roman Catholic Church alone was authentically Christian. In Europe the Church had often been a point of common identification; and in America it could serve as the apron strings which kept the newcomer tied to the heritage of the mother country. The anti-Catholic aspects of American nativism tended to keep the older immigrants attached to the Church. The militant characteristics which American Catholicism acquired during the period of the Irish inroads were a useful tool in the hands of the cadre of religious who later manned the machinery of the Church.

The most significant development of this period was that Catholic parochial schools were made mandatory. This is not to say that Catholic parochial schools were erected as a result of these school decrees. Rather the reasons for these pronouncements were also the reasons behind the parochial school system. Today, many of these reasons no longer exist and have even been forgotten, yet the mandates remain and so do the school buildings.

NOTES

1. Dana was the author of *Two Years before the Mast*. Ironically, though he could write eloquently of the wrongs done to merchant sailors, he saw no injustice in compelling children to participate in religious activities repugnant to them and to their parents.
2. Pierce vs. Society of School Sisters, 268 U.S. 510 (1925). This case was cited and praised by His Holiness, Pope Pius XI, in the encyclical *Divini illius Magistri* of 1929. *Seven Great Encyclicals,* p. 47. It is probably the only U.S. Supreme Court case to be lauded publicly in writing by a pope.
3. See Table I in the Appendix. Note the disproportionate commitment of archdioceses within the German triangle compared to those located outside the Midwest.
4. Is it possible that the degree of one's present commitment to Catholic parochial education or one's approach to present-day school problems is tempered by the extent of investment in schools by his parish, his diocese, or his general geographical area?
5. The best single source on McMaster and his role in the history of the schools is: Thomas T. McAvoy, "Public Schools vs. Catholic Schools and James McMaster," *The Review of Politics,* Volume XVIII, Number 1 (January, 1966), pp. 19–46. Much of the material in the foregoing discussion was taken from this article.

NOTES

6. This was a reference to the Apostolic Letter of Pope Pius IX entitled *Quum non sine*. The text of the letter appears in *Education: Papal Teachings*, pp. 49–53. The significant part of the text insofar as the McMaster-Edes-DePauw memorial is concerned reads: "In all places, in every country where this pernicious plan to deprive the Church of her authority over schools is formulated and, worse still, put into effect, and where youth will consequently be exposed to the danger of losing their faith, it is the serious duty of the Church to make every effort not only to obtain for youth the essential instruction and Christian training, but even more so to warn the faithful and to make it clear to them that they cannot frequent such schools as are set up against the Catholic Church." p. 52.
7. This is an interesting idea in that "victory" reflects a militancy largely unknown in American Catholicism before it became an immigrant church.
8. Some of the more reactionary elements of the conservative wing seemed to have felt that this was a dangerous encroachment on the right of the parents to educate their children in a manner they considered appropriate. The documents issued pursuant to Vatican II encourage cooperation with state certification programs.
9. Coeducation, that is, education of boys in common with girls, was long a practice traditionally deplored in Catholic circles but not forbidden by canon law.
10. "Sacramental absolution" is the remission of sins by a duly authorized priest in the sacrament of penance. Some conservatives felt that the failure of parents to send their children to Catholic schools should be made a matter of "reserved sin," that is, the right of sacramental absolution being reserved to the local bishop alone.
11. "In some respects the Instruction of 1875," writes Father McAvoy, "was the first clear American ruling on the obligation to send Catholic children to Catholic schools. In that sense James McMaster and his aide, Miss Edes, did obtain an answer to their plea, but the official silence in the United States about the Instruction and the failure to make practical applications of its rule rendered the decree nugatory at the time of its appearance . . . it is most unusual in the history of Catholicism in the United States, partly because, in this instance, the rigorists were the laity and the moderates were the archbishops and bishops of the country." *Public Schools vs. Catholic Schools and James McMaster*, p. 45. A more precise term than "laity" which McAvoy uses is "some laymen."
12. The minutes on the discussions on education, however, have been rendered into English. Francis P. Cassidy, "Catholic Education in the Third Plenary Council of Baltimore," *Catholic Historical Review*, Volume XXXIV (October, 1948 and January, 1949), pp. 257–305, 414–436. These notes are an invaluable primary source, but unfortunately Cassidy's interpretation of them is too contemporary. He tends to read the late nineteen-forties into Catholic education of the eighteen-eighties.
13. Bishop Fitzgerald was a very interesting personality. His was one of the only two dissenting votes at Vatican I in 1870 cast against the proposition on papal infallibility.
14. Robert D. Cross suggests that "the legislation of The Third Plenary Council was carefully reviewed by Roman Authorities, and the Prefect of Propaganda made it clear that the council of archbishops could never 'declare ecclesiastical law.'" In other words, a possible reason for the minor changes simply might have been to be a subtle show of power to impress upon the American hierarchy their subservient position to the Holy See. *The Emergence of Liberal Catholicism in America* (Chicago: Quadrangle Paperbacks, 1968), p. 179.

NOTES

15. The ultimate cause of the decrees and pastoral is largely a matter of interpretation. It would seem to this writer that the content of the decrees was dictated and prompted by the Vatican and bolstered by the conservative bloc in the American Church, much of which was German. The decrees were, therefore, brought about by a coalition of conservatives, the same persons and groups that were the real school builders.
16. McCluskey, p. 1. And these figures are misleadingly low if one considers the voluntary and unpaid services of the countless religious personnel and underpaid services of many lay persons over the same period of time that are not included in this estimate. For a more complete listing of school statistics see Table II in the Appendix.
17. An "ordinary" is the local bishop. The reference to "Tridentine Law" is a citation to legislation enacted at the Council of Trent which was held during the Reformation era. Peter Guilday likewise noted the strong lead that the Archdiocese of Cincinnati began to take on school issues beginning in the late 1850's, and he noted, too, the large German element there. *A History of the Councils of Baltimore,* pp. 237–238.
18. Spalding's views were somewhat unique in that he felt that good Catholic universities were the *sine qua non* of good Catholic elementary schools.
19. Frederick J. Zwerlein, *The Life and Letters of Bishop McQuaid,* 3 volumes (Rochester: The Art Print Shop, Distributing for the Louvain, 1927). This is a monumental study and provides an indispensable guide to the understanding of the conservative point of view. McQuaid was probably the dominant personality in the conservative camp.
20. This, too, is admittedly a matter of interpretation; and not all would agree that the honor goes to Ireland. Ellis feels that James Gibbons was "probably the greatest single figure the Church in the United States has produced. . . ." Ellis, *American Catholicism,* p. 104. This is a tenable nomination, but it should be remembered that it comes from the most respected biographer Gibbons has had to date. Gibbons was an accomplished politician, and his real views on certain issues were sometimes skillfully masked. Some contemporaries nicknamed him "Slippery Jim."
21. William J. McGucken, *The Catholic Way in Education* (Chicago: Loyola University Press, 1962), p. 83. This book was originally published by Bruce Publishing Company in 1934.
22. "Ablegate" is the technical name of the position held by Satolli. It is the rough equivalent of minister or delegate.
23. Faribault and Stillwater were not mentioned by name in the document.
24. Concerning "Americanism" Robert Cross writes: "With this objectification of the resentments of an unusually depressing decade of European Church history, the opposition which had been coalescing against 'religious Americanism' was completed. Joined with the hysteria-ridden were deeply religious men who disliked the activist, self-confident, apparently worldly tone the liberals gave to Catholicism; ultramontanes indignant at the revival of a spirit they thought had finally been scotched at the Vatican Council; French monarchists who detested Ireland for his forthright endorsement of the Third Republic; Spaniards who resented American assertions that a progressive church and state could accomplish in a few years for Cuba and the Philippines what three hundred years of Spanish endeavor had failed to do; Germans anxious to win just treatment for their countrymen in America; Jesuits who treasured corporate as well as ideological antagonisms to the American hierarchy. Under direct attack from so many Catholics, the Americanists lost the privilege which, as

NOTES

pioneers achieving unusual success in an unusually large task, they had long enjoyed to deviate from the pattern of ultramontane Catholicism. As a result, in the decade of the 1890's the Americans received not the grateful recognition they expected but a series of official rebukes. The interplay of personalities and institutions in Rome markedly affected the phrasing and timing of the several declarations, but, taken together, the reprimands left no room for doubt that responsible authorities, including Leo XIII, had formed an unfavorable opinion of the direction toward which the American liberals seemed to be tending." *The Emergence of Liberal Catholicism in America,* p. 195.

25. Quoted in Thomas T. McAvoy, *The Americanist Heresy in Roman Catholicism, 1895–1900* (Notre Dame, Indiana: Notre Dame University Press, 1963), pp. 256–257.
26. William Torrey Harris was a famous school superintendent in Saint Louis who became United States Commissioner of Education from 1889 to 1906. Ella Flagg Young was superintendent in Chicago from 1909 to 1915.
27. Leo XIII, Encyclical *Immortale Dei* (The Christian Constitution of the States), November 1, 1885, in Gerald F. Yates (ed.), *Papal Thought on the State: Excerpts from Encyclicals and Other Writings of Recent Popes* (New York: Appleton-Century-Crofts, Inc., 1958), pp. 12–29.
28. Leo XIII, Encyclical *Libertas Praestantissimum* (On Human Liberty), June 20, 1888, in Yates, pp. 30–52.
29. Leo XIII, Letter *Quod in novissimo,* April 10, 1887, to James Gibbons, in *Education: Papal Teachings,* p. 103.
30. "Catholic philosophy" is a term Catholics often hear. Many priests like to use it, so do nuns; and some Catholic laymen like it too. It would seem that one should be able to define "Catholic philosophy" with ease; but, when one takes time to consider it more seriously, he discovers, perhaps to his surprise, that it is a very confusing and very vague term. It is defined by some in terms of realism, by others in terms of idealism, and still others in terms of existentialism. One might reasonably conclude from this that there is not really a "Catholic philosophy," but, more accurately, there are only "Catholic philosophers."

IV
The Golden Era
1919–1958

It was World War I more than any specific papal or hierarchical effort that brought an end to the disunity in the Church that had posed a constant menace since at least the end of the Civil War era. The peace achieved at the Third Plenary Council of Baltimore had been artificial, superficial, and short-lived; but that achieved by organizing to win the war was enduring because the passage of immigration restriction quotas in the 1920's prevented it from breaking apart in squabbles over "Americanization" and foreignism.[1] The 1920's were a time of revived nativism. The relative calm within the Church was a contrast to the climate outside of the Church; it was a period of intense anti-Catholic feeling, especially in the South, Southwest, and even in some midwestern states such as Indiana. There was an increase in membership in the Ku Klux Klan and a whole spate of new cross burnings. Religion was also an important political issue in the presidential campaigns of 1924 and 1928. In 1928 the Democratic nomination went to Alfred E. Smith of New York, a Roman Catholic. The only other Catholic to have received the nomination of a major party in American history is John F. Kennedy. Smith was defeated by Herbert Hoover by a wide margin. His religion was not his only handicap, however, as the question of prohibition complicated the issue. Smith had little formal schooling, and his lack of finesse as a public speaker could be detected over the radio which, by this time, brought the voice of the candidates into millions of American homes. The

The Golden Era

Democrats would have had a difficult time winning with any standard bearer as they were running against eight years of Republican prosperity, but Smith was a strong candidate. He reflected the growing Catholic influence in politics, especially urban politics. It is hard to assess the precise impact of all these influences on the Catholic parochial school movement. It probably tended to keep the peace within the Catholic camp, and it may have convinced many Catholic parents that public schools would be too anti-Catholic for their children. One good thing often resulting from a "persecution complex," whether the grounds for it are real or imagined, is that it keeps the "persecuted" united to meet the real or imagined enemy.

Ninety-three members of the hierarchy met in Washington in September, 1919, and one of the results of their conference was the first national pastoral letter since 1884. It was probably written for the bishops by Father Edward Pace of the faculty of the Catholic University and signed by the aged Cardinal Gibbons. Some parts of it were grandiloquent, but the general goals outlined in it were laudable. Lasting peace, read the letter, will come about by educating "youth toward a complete understanding of their duties. Herein lies the importance of education and the responsibility of those to whom it is entrusted." In another passage suggestive of the biblical distinction between wisdom and knowledge, the bishops said "of itself knowledge gives no guarantee that it will issue righteous action . . . therefore . . . it is still more necessary to insure that all educational activity shall be guided by sound principles toward the attainment of its true purpose." In what would soon become almost a leitmotif, the bishops observed that Catholics had to bear a burden of double taxation, that is, they had to pay public school taxes while at the same time supporting their own parochial schools. Apparently they did not envison public funding of the secular aspects of instruction or shared and released time to be measures to alleviate this "injustice" because they also stated that "moral and religious training is most efficacious when it is joined with instructions in other kinds of knowledge. It should so permeate these that its influence will be felt in every circumstance. . . ." The bishops seemed to have felt that a truly good education could not be secular. In reference to the parochial school system in the United States they declared that "our own Catholic schools are not established and maintained with any idea of holding our children apart from the general body and spirit of American citizenship. They are simply the concrete form in which we exercise our rights as free citizens, in conformity with the dictates of conscience. Their very existence is a great moral fact in America."[2] Compared with earlier pastoral letters, the section on education in that of 1919 was rather lengthy, but it dealt in generalities and really contained nothing that had not been said earlier. In that year there were 5,788 parochial schools in the country with an enrollment of 1,633,599. The total Roman Catholic population in the United States stood at just over 17,500,000 persons.

Pope Benedict, who had succeeded Pius X in 1914, died in 1922. Perhaps the most enduring of the legacies of his pontificate was the completion of the new code of canon law which had been begun by his predecessor. It did much to clarify the roles of various ecclesiastical functionaries and solidify the centralization that had occurred in the Church in the previous hundred years. It was, one might almost say, the finalizing of the great concessions to ultramontanism. The *Codex* was a massive and complex body of writings, and the bishops had to rely more and more on priests with a facility in Latin and extensive training in Church law to interpret its dictates. The excesses of legalism that sometimes resulted, joined with the effects of the earlier decree on Modernism, the censorship of published materials, the checks on permission for priests and religious to write and speak publicly, the rigidness of the typical seminary curriculum, and the initial educational poverty of the typical immigrant—all of these things—helped to account for the generally low intellectual achievement in the American Church in the next decades. Certainly the Church's necessary preoccupation with education at the lower level to "Americanize" the immigrant diminished Catholic efforts at higher levels. Catholics did not produce a number of professional persons and scholars commensurate with their percentage of the total national population.

Books and other published materials were censored by the Church in two ways. First, any publications concerned with matters of faith or morals were to be submitted to specially appointed diocesan authorities for examination for doctrinal errors. Clearance for publication was indicated by the term *nihil obstat* imprinted near the title page which meant "nothing obstructs." This meant no errors were found by the censor. With this was to be included an *imprimatur* which meant "it may be printed," and this was to be issued by the bishop. These devices were designed to prevent the printing of objectionable materials. A second censorship device was concerned with printed materials not submitted for pre-publication review. Any such materials found highly objectionable could be placed on the Index of Prohibited Books, a list of forbidden reading materials. Disregard of the Church's laws regarding the publishing, reading, selling, or even possession of certain types of materials could bring penalties ranging all the way to excommunication. Books on the Index or lacking an *imprimatur* were not to be used in Catholic schools. Theoretically intended only as an assurance of doctrinal orthodoxy, the canons on censorship were applied differently by various bishops. It was easier to get an *imprimatur* in certain dioceses than in others.

Pope Pius XI, who succeeded Benedict XV, had been the Archbishop of Milan before assuming the papal throne. In some ways his reign was marked by the most difficult crises the Vatican had had to face since Napoleon took Pius VII a prisoner. Pius XI ascended the throne about the time Mussolini came into power in Italy; and he died in 1939, six years after Hitler had taken over in Germany. Not only did his administration have to contend with fascism but also with a world-wide economic depression of unprecedented magnitude. It was toward the middle of his pontificate that Pope Pius XI issued his famous encyclical *Divini illius Magistri* (Christian Education of Youth).[3] It is the lengthiest recent papal statement on education. Synthesizing all previous official pronouncements, it has become the reference point for any discussion of the position of the Roman Catholic Church on education.

Unlike most earlier statements made by popes about education, Pius' encyclical addressed the entire Church and not just Catholics in a particular country or a specific prelate. Much of the letter dealt in philosophical principles, and its style might be best described as Victorian. The Pope said he wrote the letter in response to many requests for a clear statement of sound educational principles. "Christian education," he said, ". . . aims at securing the Supreme Good, that is, God, for the souls of those who are being educated, and the maximum of well-being possible here below for human society." There are three basic societies in the world, he went on, namely, the Church, the family, and the State. "Education which is concerned with man as a whole, individually and socially, in order of nature and in the order of grace, necessarily belongs to all these societies, in due proportion, corresponding according to the dispositions of Divine Providence, to the co-ordination of their respective ends." The Pope stated that "education belongs pre-eminently to the Church" because when Jesus said "teach ye all nations" he conferred upon the Church a magisterial office and because of this the Church must educate men in the ways of salvation. The Church is consequently independent of anything temporal but nevertheless is willing to cooperate with the legitimate dispositions of the State. "It is the inalienable right as well as the indispensible duty of the Church," concluded Pope Pius XI, "to watch over the entire education of her children, in all institutions, public or private, not merely in regard to religious instruction there given, but in regard to every other branch of learning and every regulation insofar as religion and morality are concerned."

As regarded the rights of the family in the realm of education, wrote the Pope, they come before any rights of the State: "The function . . . of civil authority residing in the State is twofold, to protect and to foster, but by no means to absorb the family and the individual, or to substitute itself for them." The State, declared the Holy Father, ought to begin its educational activities by supplementing the work of the Church and family. "Unjust and unlawful is any monoply, educational or scholastic, which, physically or morally, forces families to make use of government schools, contrary to the dictates of their Christian conscience, or contrary to their legitimate preference," he went on. And he also praised the United States Supreme Court decision of 1925 which ruled unconstitutional an Oregon state law compelling all children to attend public schools. Some persons might counter the Pope's remarks here with the observation that during the Middle Ages, before the Reformation made signboards in front of churches a necessity, the Roman Church held a virtual monopoly on education. Monastery schools, cathedral schools, chantries, convents, parish schools, and even guilds were largely controlled by the Church; but one distinction should be made between the year 1429 and 1929. In the former year compulsory attendance laws which required every child to attend some sort of school did not exist. It must be observed, too, that Pius expressed little concern about the education of non-Catholic children. What was to become of the Protestant or Jewish child attending the "ideal" school that was permeated with Roman Catholic piety?

Possibly one of the most fundamental concepts of "Catholic educational philosophy" is the idea of original sin. "Every method of education," stated Pope Pius XI, "founded, wholly or in part, on the denial or forgetfulness of original sin and of grace and relying on the sole powers of human nature, is unsound."[4] Pius went on to depreciate any systems of educational philosophy which are based only on the "purely natural and profane order." Man has a fallen nature; man has been redeemed; man must be taught the way to avail himself of the saving grace of Jesus Christ. Methods and models of education which forget these central facts are false. Such systems typically foster "a pretended self-government and unrestrained freedom on the part of the child, and . . . diminish or even suppress the teacher's authority and action, attributing to the child an exclusive primacy of initiative, and an activity independent of any higher law, natural or divine, in the work of his education." Calvin had said the child was totally depraved; Rousseau, that the child was good but corrupted by human institutions; and Dewey, that the child was neutral. Pius said the child had a fallen nature redeemed by Christ.

Pope Pius XI also expressed his disapproval of many forms of sex education. ". . . In young people, evil practices are the effect not so much of ignorance of intellect as of weakness of a will exposed to dangerous occasions, and unsupported by means of grace." His Holiness also argued that coeducation was wrong, that boys should be educated apart from girls. Father William McGucken, a rather well-known Jesuit educational philosopher during the 1930's, drew up plans for a utopian school based on this encyclical letter of Pope Pius XI's. In his school, McGucken said he would rigidly enforce the rule of the separation of the sexes. "If there be one who takes exception on the view of coeducation here expressed," Father McGucken admonished, "he is perfectly free to abandon this part of the plan, although he should be warned that his educational system will be, by that much imperfect. The encyclical of Pope Pius XI *On Christian Education* might also be quoted merely to prove to the skeptic that the writer [namely, McGucken himself] in opposing coeducation is only holding to Catholic tradition. His Holiness does not hesitate to condemn coeducation. . . ."[5] In insisting that the essence of sex education was will training, the Pope was consistent in his philosophy with other comments he made about curriculum. The Holy Father, as did his immediate predecessors and successors, seemed to subscribe to faculty psychology, which was really more of a philosophy of learning than anything else. Faculty psychology was not new with the popes; indeed it was at least as old as the Greeks. Faculty psychologists envisioned the mind as divided into a fixed number of compartments, or functions, or faculties—for example, memory, imagination, reasoning, intuition, and will power. Development of one of these faculties by hard work and practice, one might say by intellectual exercise, would lead to a better facility in the overall use of this faculty. The popes, while never openly expressing their belief in faculty psychology, nevertheless showed that they subscribed to it by their discussions on curriculum and educational methodology. The remarks of Pius XI on sex education and also on the value of Latin as a school subject are typical of the genre.

The Pope, while not contradicting any earlier writings on education, appeared to take a harder line on cooperation with public schools than had Leo XIII in his *tolerari potest*.[6] He opposed schools in which religion was excluded altogether and those where Catholics were educated in common with non-Catholics. He also disapproved of providing students with separate religious instruction but permitting them to receive all other lessons with non-Catholic pupils and from non-Catholic teachers. For a school to be "a fit place for Catholic students," said the Pope, ". . . it is necessary that all the teaching and the whole organization of the school, and its teachers, syllabus and textbooks in every branch, be regulated by the Christian spirit, under the direction and maternal supervision of the Church; so that religion may be in very truth the foundation and crown of the youth's training; and this in every grade of school, not only elementary, but the intermediate and higher institutions of learning as well." In his contemporary evaluation of the letter, Father McGucken said "it would be absurd to say that the Pope approves of the [American] public school system." These remarks of Pius XI would appear to refute arguments of those proponents of public aid to parochial education who insist that the State should subsidize the teaching of secular subjects as the Pope seems to have been saying that there was no such thing. He favored direct grants to private education, and he said that Roman

The Golden Era

Catholics "in agitating for Catholic schools for their children, are not mixing in party politics, but are engaged in a religious enterprise demanded by conscience." He might have been willing to make the same remarks about agitating for public financial assistance for these schools. The concluding sections of the encyclical *Divini illius Magistri* of 1929 are somewhat homiletic with frequent references to the Bible, to some of the Roman classics, and to Saint Augustine.

The Pope's statement was a conservative one to say the least. It really added nothing that had not been said previously. Some might argue that the statement was a move by the Pope into educational theory—theology and philosophy of education—to a degree that had not occurred previously. Much of what he said regarding the proper pedagogy to be used in the education of youth went beyond strict doctrine. The encyclical is most understandable if one considers and judges it in the context of the times. A reaction on the part of the Vatican to contemporary events in Fascist Italy, Nazi Germany, and Soviet Russia, the encyclical really received "little more than lip service in its specific application to the American scene."[7] For instance, forty-eight percent of the Catholic high schools in the United States in 1966 were coeducational despite the fact that the encyclical was still quoted and praised.[8] Pius issued many other statements on educational topics, but their content and tone were entirely consistent with the *Divini illius Magistri*.

The twenties were good years for the Catholic parochial schools. In 1920 there were approximately 5,800 institutions; in 1930, 7,200, or a gain of 1,400 schools. In the first fifty years of this century, the rate of Catholic school construction has closely paralleled the general state of the national economy. The good times of the twenties were followed by the depression years and World War II, both of which cut into parochial school enrollments and building programs. In 1933 the actual number of Catholic parish elementary schools decreased. This is the first decrease recorded since the statistics became available in 1875, and it may well be the first decrease to have occurred in the history of the schools. The number of schools continued to go down until 1939. The recovery period was short-lived as World War II seemed to cause another dip in the number of schools in 1943 and 1944. Even more revealing are the statistics on enrollments. There were approximately 2,300,000 youngsters enrolled in 1935, and then came the depression and war declines. The high figure was not equalled again until 1949, but, then, it should be noted that there were six million more Roman Catholics in the United States so that, while the 1949 enrollment figures are comparable to those of 1935 in absolute terms, they represent a relative loss.

By this time nuns had almost completely replaced brothers in parochial school classrooms. There were literally scores of teaching communities, the major ones including the Franciscans, Dominicans, Benedictines, and Josephites. It was extremely rare to find a grade school staffed by a religious community of men. Brothers were more frequently found teaching in Catholic high schools. The vast numbers of women who taught in religious habit for minimal wages were the *sine qua non* of the parochial school system. Some of the more reactionary elements, like McGucken, lamented the fact that boys were being taught by nuns instead of men but the trend was irreversible.

The bishops of the twenties, thirties, and forties tended to be extremely conservative, perhaps still owing to the condemnation of Modernism. The pronouncements made by the Administrative Committee of the National Catholic Welfare Conference[9] in Washignton, D.C. reflected this conservatism and did not appreciably vary in tone from the *Divini illius Magistri*. These statements, while not so authoritative as pastoral letters, are significant and indicative of the general prevailing mood. In 1933 the bishops wrote that the public schools were keeping many idle youths from the ranks of the unemployed and were consequently doing something that would be better done by industry. They also stated that "our Catholic schools . . . see the folly of attempting to rival the extravagantly conducted tax-paid schools and of regarding them as norms of perfection." The idea that all public schools are fabulously well equipped is a misconception still held by many Catholics. Despite their supposedly lavish appointments, the bishops apparently did not think too highly of these public schools as they also stated that "our difficulties today are largely efforts to remedy the evils inevitable in any system of education that permits chaotic thinking, pagan license, and uncurbed greed to take the place of that necessary discipline in thought and conduct that produces worthy and upright lives."

The famous encyclical of Pope Pius XI's was issued in the same year that the Stock Market crash occurred. The Catholic Church in

America felt the pains of the resulting depression as did almost everyone and everything else. Catholic leaders of the time of John Hughes had favored some form of public aid to church schools; but, during the nativist agitation of the 1880's and 1890's, many became less vocal in their demands for such assistance. In fact some of them, true to the generally conservative temper of the times, were opposed in principle to government aid. Before the era of the New Deal, then, most Catholic spokesmen were opposed to federal aid to education, but between 1934 and 1939 there appears to have been a shift from this position to one of "qualified support for federal aid to education—provided children in parochial schools could share in its benefits."[10] It would appear that there was another shift in the 1950's. The Catholic Church in America today is more militant, even aggressive, in its lobby efforts for public aid. One person who may have been responsible for this was the late Monsignor Frederick Hockwalt, Executive Secretary of the National Catholic Education Association. This, however, is a story of which historians have yet to tell. It is worthy of note that the bishops, though lobbying for government aid to church schools, have never really polled the opinion of the rank and file of the laity on the subject.

In 1944 the Department of Education of the National Catholic Welfare Conference issued a statement on the question of federal aid for Catholic schools. It was really a rather timid document if judged by present standards. In it the members of the Department publicly declared their opposition to the creation of a federal bureau for education as a cabinet level agency, to federal control of education, and, interestingly enough, to aid of any form "which cannot be demonstrated as needed to meet the minimum educational requirements in areas where resources are inadequate." In addition, they made several recommendations: that federal aid be given only where absolutely necessary to all accredited schools without regard to race, national origin, or religious affiliation; that federal aid supplement but never supplant local and state efforts; and that federal assistance be given without the imposition of government controls. The position had changed from opposition to aid to an insistance that aid, if given, should be made available to Catholic as well as public schools.

Programs for aid to parochial schools have not consisted exclusively of plans for outright grants. Since the Cochran Case in 1930, when the Supreme Court upheld the state of Louisiana's "loan" of textbooks to parochial schools, similar programs have been sustained in other states. The basis of the court's reasoning was the "child benefit theory," that is, the gift was considered to have been made for the individual student and not for the Church. The same line of reasoning has been applied and sustained by the courts with regard to public financing of the busing of parochial school children. The federal government has also applied the same reasoning to justify its hot lunch programs, some of its health programs, and, of course, the 1965 Elementary and Secondary Education Act (ESEA). Shared-time programs, however, have not been sustained though released-time programs have been upheld.

The hierarchy continued to issue statements through the Administrative Board from time to time. One of the more interesting of these, though touching upon education only indirectly, did so in a rather significant way. The statement in question was concerned with the authority and importance of papal encyclicals and was issued in 1936, seven years after *Divini illius Magistri*. Part of the problems then confronting the world, wrote the prelates, could have been averted if the teachings of the popes in their encyclicals had been heeded. "Every word in these encyclicals," they continued, "brings into the clearest light the accuracy with which the popes diagnosed the ills of society and the sureness with which they prescribed the most effective remedies. These encyclicals were issued to check the devastating course of the forces of error and disorder. . . . There is no evil of the present . . . which has not been analyzed and evaluated in these authoritative utterances of the supreme pontiffs."

One of the common themes in the writings of the period by the hierarchy was that public schools were undesirable because they were secular and that Catholic schools were a necessary counterbalance in society. "In no field," stated the American hierarchy in 1947, "has secularism done more harm than in education." A year later their official statement read: "At a time when secularism has captured the minds of very many leaders in education, it is heartening that Catholic parents are becoming more insistent in their demands for schools in which the best standards of instruction and training are integrated in the teaching of religion." In 1950, they praised those who supported parochial schools, endorsed released-time programs, and urged parents who could not take advantage of Catholic schools to send their children to Sunday schools and vacation schools. The remarks approving of released time are most intriguing. Pope Pius XI had clearly expressed his disapproval of such programs in his 1929 encyclical letter though it is probably most accurate to say that he did not actually condemn them. But the bishops, acting through the same body which uttered the statement on released time, had already praised the encyclicals of the popes as "authoritative" statements in which "every word" had significance. Was this a shift in position? It sometimes appears that the American bishops do not read the letters written by their predecessors. The pastorals and other writings of the hierarchy, if considered as a whole from the time of John Carroll, are replete with contradictions. Shifts in position might explain some of these inconsistencies but they are more likely the results of a failure on the part of drafting committees to gather together and read carefully the earlier documents before composing new documents.

One of the more colorful incidents of the era was the feud between Eleanor Roosevelt and Cardinal Spellman of New York triggered by the school issue.[11] In her syndicated newspaper column of June 23, 1949, Mrs. Roosevelt stated that "those of us who believe in the right of any human being to belong to whatever church he sees fit, and to worship God in his own way, cannot be accused of prejudice when we do not want to see public education connected with religious control of the schools, which are paid for by taxpayers' money." Spellman responded to the editorial with a blistering letter, dated July 21; and it read in part:

> 'Taxation without representation is tyranny' was the cry that roused and rallied our pioneer Americans to fight for justice. *Taxation without participation* [emphases Spellman's] should rouse today's Americans to equal ardor to protest an injustice that would deprive millions of American children of health and safety benefits to which all our children are entitled....
>
> ...why I wonder do you repeatedly plead causes that are anti-Catholic? Even if you cannot find it in your heart to defend the rights of innocent little children... can you not have the charity not to cast upon them still another stone?

And he continued:

> For, whatever you may say in the future, your record of anti-Cathol-

icism stands for all to see—a record which you yourself wrote on the pages of history which cannot be recalled—documents of discrimination unworthy of an American mother!

Needless to say the remarks of His Eminence caused a national sensation. They were without precedent in American history. An American prelate had labelled a former First Lady as a bigot, a woman who had enjoyed something of a reputation for being a humanitarian. Many found it hard to see how the woman who had come to the defense of Marian Anderson could be the blackguard the Cardinal described. Spellman was one of the most influential prelates in the American Church at the time. He was Archbishop of New York and Vicar Apostolic of the Armed Forces, and he enjoyed warm and close personal relations with the reigning Pope, Pius XII. In many ways his personality was reminiscent of that of his predecessor John Hughes. In philosophic outlook, however, he was very akin to another predecessor, namely, Archbishop Corrigan; but he had a charisma Corrigan had lacked and John Ireland possessed. In Mrs. Roosevelt, Spellman had found his match. She felt that the Cardinal had misconstrued her motives and her position, and she was too shrewd to get into a public epistolary duel with the Archbishop. Her letter of response was a gem. Dated July 23, 1949, it read in part: "I assure you that I have no sense of being 'an unworthy American mother.' The final judgment, my dear Cardinal Spellman, of the unworthiness of all human beings is in the hands of God." While Cardinal Spellman's remarks were downright intemperate, the most that could be said for the First Lady's was that they were patronizing. Most Americans probably viewed her as the winner in the episode but most bishops sided with Spellman and the majority of Catholics shared his sentiments, too.

The official position of the Church, one that was accepted in virtually all Catholic circles in the late forties and early fifties, was that all education should be religious in orientation and controlled by the Church. Cardinal Spellman in remarks uttered on an occasion that was not so charged with emotion said that "passing through this archdiocese [namely, New York] and looking down on it from the air church after church is seen and near the church, the school. . . . Erected with the voluntary contributions of the people, they are one glory of the Church. They represent faith, consecration, sacrifice and progress." These words expressed the great consensus of American Catholics at that time. The schools had become a source of great pride to most of them. Most Protestants and Jews, quite understandably, objected to the idea of religious control of all education. Some advocated instead complete separation of the religious element from the secular with the former taught by the church or synagogue and the latter by the public school. This viewpoint was the prevalent one as public schools were for the most part secular institutions by the forties and fifties. This aspect is what Spellman and others considered most objectionable in them. Catholics of earlier generations had not found public schools to be secular but rather nondenominational Protestant and sometimes very anti-Catholic. It is interesting to speculate whether the German conservative faction would have been successful in 1884 had the public schools been of the cast of those sixty years later. There were many Protestants of the middle years of the twentieth century who still felt that religion ought to be taught in the public schools because it was a part of the American culture, but Jews as well as Catholics were generally opposed to this as they thought that any such instruction would inevitably be some brand of Protestant Christianity. Shared and released time found adherents and opponents in all groups.

The period immediately following World War II were boom years for the Catholic school system. The effects of the virtual end to immigration could be seen in the Church. The traditional rancor that had existed between the newcomers and "Americanized" churches was largely a thing of the past. The Catholic school system which was the product of this tension, a legacy of an earlier era, survived and was entering into a time of expansion. The birthrate rose at the end of the war, and the overall prosperity of the economy put Catholics in a position where they could pay for a parochial school education. What was even more important was that many Catholics wanted such an education for their youngsters. Many prelates and persons in places of power in Catholic education continually fail to distinguish between could and would. Financial crises in Catholic schools can have two causes: Catholics do not have sufficient means to contribute to their support; Catholics have adequate resources but are unwilling to share them. The late forties, the fifties, and the early sixties were the golden age of the parochial school system because the faithful were willing and able. Between 1940 and 1960, the number of Catholic schools increased by at least fifty percent; and the enrollment doubled. The number of Catholic schools between World War II and 1960 increased faster than the number of public schools. By 1960, the total number of parochial schools was about ten thousand. Lost in all the numbers, however, was a crucial fact many Catholic educational leaders too often overlooked. The increase was only one of numbers. With each passing year, the proportion of Catholics actually attending Catholic schools was declining. One possible reason for this may have been that the "Americanization" of the Catholic immigrant was nearly completed. The school system had to depend for its existence on the strength of the parochial school custom among American Catholics and on sheer force of ecclesiastical law.

The fifties were marked by rather intense educational reforms. Possibly many of these educational developments of the period might have come about sooner had it not been for the Depression and World War II. After 1945, the greater numbers of birth and the "surplus" funds that were no longer committed to the military effort acted as catalysts, and the Russian launching of Sputnik in 1957 gave added impetus to the movement. The Catholic schools were caught up in the temper of the times as were the public schools. The great interest in education was reflected in a number of research projects into the nature and problems of Catholic education, and there was a spate of what one might consider "Catholic Conant Reports."[12] There was also a concomitant effort to upgrade the quality of Catholic education. Part of this entailed a broadening of the curriculum. Catholic schools traditionally stressed the liberal arts and languages. The majority of teachers were religious, and these were the areas stressed in seminary and convent schools. It was only natural that the clergy consider especially important those subject areas in which they were interested and trained, but the increasing national emphasis on science and mathematics had an effect on the Catholic school curriculum. Team teaching, non-graded schools, audiovisual technology, centralization of administration, teacher unionization, and all the other concerns of public school reformers likewise have been the concerns of Catholic educators.

One especially important trend in Catholic education during the fifties was the shift in staff composition. Nuns continued to be the backbone of the system though an increasing number of lay teachers was employed with each passing year. The percentage of lay teachers increased perhaps as much as four times between 1950 and 1960. By 1970 nearly half the Catholic school teachers were laymen. The era also witnessed many reform movements within the Catholic sisterhoods. More often than not these were initiated by the nuns themselves, and one of their goals was to improve the professional training of sister-teachers. The idea that reform in the convents was started with Vatican II is a myth.

There were three pontiffs between 1919 and 1958. The writings on education of the first two of these, Benedict XV and Pius XI, have already been analyzed. Eugenio Pacelli, who became Pope in 1939, had visited the United States a few years before his elevation and was the first pope who had ever been to America. His pontificate was a rather long one lasting more than nineteen years. He was a tall and slender man with a commanding presence. His personality was austere, but he was extremely popular in his own lifetime. He issued no comprehensive statement on education that was comparable to the encyclical *Divini illius Magistri,* but many of his letters and allocutions contained short segments on education. Early in his reign, for instance, he issued the encyclical *Sertum Laetitiae* commemorating the one hundred and fiftieth anniversary of the founding of the American hierarchy. In this letter, the Pope praised the work of the bishops of the United States, of religious orders, of the National Catholic Welfare Conference, and of Catholic University in Washington, D. C. On the negative side of the ledger, he denounced birth control and warned against a public school system from which religion was excluded. The likely result, he said, would be a "sorrowful harvest in the intellectual and moral life of the nation."

The general body of educational statements of Pope Pius XII were quite consistent and in keeping with the conservative tone set by his predecessors. He was in accord with the sentiments expressed in the *Divini illius Magistri.* He felt that it was of permanent value and quoted it frequently. His statements on education ranged over many topics. For instance, like his predecessors he valued Latin in the curriculum.[13] He considered the religious life superior to lay life and felt that one of the great values of Catholic schools was that they inculcated religious vocations. He thought it was essential for parochial school teachers to be good Catholics but also to have a good professional preparation. The Pope also felt that the education of the very young ought to be left to women. Pius approved of the parochial school system as it had developed in America, and he was convinced that there was no justifiable reason why any Catholic school had to be in any way inferior to a public institution.

Late in 1958, Pius XII died and was succeeded by Angelo Roncalli, Patriarch of Venice, who assumed the name John XXIII. The new Pope was of an entirely different cut than his predecessors of the preceding hundred years. His reign coincides with the beginning of a new era, one that was to see marked changes in the American parochial school system.

* * *

The forty-year period in the history of the American Catholic parochial schools spanning the years 1919 to 1958 might be viewed as an epoch and labelled the "Golden Era" just as the periods before 1919 might be called the "Era of the Germans," "Era of the Irish," and "Era of the English." Unlike any previous period, this was not marked by any mass immigration, and the various ethnic groups began to become assimilated into the mainstream of the American culture. The existence of the Catholic schools was accepted as a necessary fact of life by the vast majority of the faithful, and within the Church itself there was no school controversy as there had been in the 1880's and 1890's. The support of the schools became more consistent throughout the various parts of the country and now seemed to be based more on financial ability than on ethnicity. This was the "Golden Age" because the general support for the schools was the broadest, the most intense, the most unquestioning, and because the school system was approaching its zenith in terms of absolute size.

The seeds for the decline of the system had already been sown and were apparent. For example, with each passing year the great desire to preserve the immigrant subculture was becoming less and less. Also, the public schools were no longer anti-Catholic. It is a matter of interpretation whether they were merely nondenominational or truly secular and nonreligious. The bishops and clergy repeatedly insisted that public schools were godless; but, despite their exhortations, the percentage of Roman Catholic youngsters in public schools was growing year after year, especially after the onset of the Great Depression.

The actual number of children being educated in the Catholic parochial system was nevertheless very large. There was a serious effort on the part of the Church authorities to see that this education was a good one, and there can be no doubt that the overall contribution of the system to the American culture was a very positive and significant one.

The writings of the popes of the period on education were numerous but almost never addressed to specific problems on the American scene. Without any doubt whatsoever, the most significant document was the 1929 encyclical letter of Pope Pius XI entitled *Divini illius Magistri*. All other pontifical writings of the era are consistent with it. The *Divini illius Magistri* was widely read in America, and, when practicable, an attempt was made to implement the philosophy it outlined.

The statements of the bishops were generally issued through committees. They do not appear to have been as significant as those of the period immediately preceding. They reflect no real leadership or innovativeness on the part of the American hierarchy. Reasons for this might have been the now ingrained and unquestioning habit of relying on Rome for direction and also the understandable preoccupation with the problems stemming from the Depression and the war and reconstruction.

The most significant developments of this period were the "Americanization" of Catholics in the United States and the relative decline in the number of children attending Catholic schools although the absolute increase during the era tended to mask this. The parochial school system was headed for foreseeable difficulties that were, unfortunately, overlooked in the halcyon days of the fifties.

NOTES

1. Frank Reuter would appear to hold that a more lasting unity was achieved earlier. He writes: "The 'splendid war' of 1898 forced the Roman Catholic Church in the United States to come of age. The Church had to throw off its tinge of foreignism and do more than merely accomodate itself to American society. To keep control of its destiny it had to reverse its traditional role of indifference to national affairs and try instead to influence the direction of national policies. How well it enacted this reversal depended on how well its members became conscious of themselves and of their numbers as a potential influence on political matters." *Catholic Influence on American Colonial Policies,* 1898–1904 (Austin, Texas: University of Texas Press, 1967), p. 35.
2. Unless noted otherwise all references to official writings of the American hierarchy from 1919 to 1950 are taken from: Raphael M. Huber, *Our Bishops Speak* (Milwaukee: Bruce Publishing Company, 1952).
3. The following references to this letter are taken from: Pius XI, *Encyclical Divini illius Magistri* in *Seven Great Encyclicals,* pp. 37–68. The letter also appears under the title "Education and the Redeemed Man" in *Education: Papal Teachings,* pp. 200–248.
4. According to traditional Roman Catholic belief, original sin is the sin committed by Adam and passed on to every human being since with the two exceptions of Jesus and Mary. Though the sin itself can be removed by the sacrament of Baptism, the consequences of the sin remain in the world, namely, vice, ignorance, and death.
5. McGucken, pp. 52–53.
6. *"Tolerari potest,"* that is, "it is tolerable," was the expression used by Leo XIII with regard to Archbishop John Ireland's shared-time programs at Stillwater and Faribault.
7. Ambrose A. Clegg, Jr., "Church Groups and Federal Aid to Education," *History of Education Quarterly,* Volume IV, Number 3 (September, 1964), p. 137.
8. Reginald A. Neuwien (ed.), *Catholic Schools in Action: The Notre Dame Study of Catholic Elementary and Secondary Schools in the United States* (Notre Dame, Indiana: Notre Dame University Press, 1966), p. 49.
9. The National Catholic Welfare Conference (NCWC) is a voluntary association of the American bishops originally formed in 1919 to serve as a central agency for organizing and coordinating various Church activities. Leadership of the NCWC rests in the Administrative Committee, or Board, which is composed of a select number of bishops and archbishops. The official statements of the NCWC between 1919 and 1950 are also in Huber.
10. Clegg, pp. 137–154.
11. The materials in the following discussion are taken from Robert I. Gannon, *The Cardinal Spellman Story* (London: Robert Hale, Ltd., 1963), pp. 314–320.
12. James Conant, a former President of Harvard, was commissioned to do a study of American high schools during the post-Sputnik furor and to come to some positive conclusions regarding remedies to end their major deficiencies. For instance: Joseph H. Fichter, *Parochial School: A Sociological Study* (Notre Dame, Indiana: Notre Dame University Press, 1958). Andrew M. Greeley and Peter H. Rossi, *The Education of Catholic Americans* (New York: Anchor Books, 1968). Sister Mary Janet, *Catholic Secondary Education: A National Survey* (Washington, D.C.: National Catholic Welfare Conference, 1949). Neuwien, *Catholic Schools in Action.*
13. An excellent source for contemporary papal statements and writing is the periodical *The Pope Speaks* which dates from 1954.

V
The Era Of The Americans
1958 — — — —

In October, 1958 Pope Pius XII died at Castelgandolfo, his summer residence. His successor was Angelo Roncalli, the aged Cardinal Patriarch of Venice, who took the name John XXIII. Though few realized it at the time, one era in the history of the Roman Catholic Church was ending and another was about to begin. John was in many ways the antithesis of Pius. He was short and heavy-set whereas Pius was tall and slender. John was gregarious; Pius, aloof and aesthetic. John gave the impression of coming from peasant stock; Pius, of being an aristocrat. But John's common sense and his political astuteness have too often been confused for liberalism. He was a traditionalist who shrewdly assayed the temper of the times and paved the way for the inevitable. He was hardly a revolutionary.

The statements of Pope John XXIII on education did not markedly differ in content from those of his immediate predecessors though they were somewhat softer in tone. Like Pius XII, he considered the 1929 encyclical *Divini illius Magistri* to be a laudable and quote-worthy statement on Christian education. Like so many of his predecessors, John favored a classical curriculum that included a strong dose of Latin and "similar disciplines." He also felt that the course of studies offered in Catholic schools ought to be a broad one and include athletics and technical training. On a theme reminiscent of earlier papal statements, John spoke of the tasks of the Christian school. "Sometimes," said His Holiness, "the tasks will be to preserve from false doctrine children and adolescents who must attend non-Catholic schools; in any event, it will always be necessary to balance the humanistic and technological education offered by the public schools with a formation based on spiritual values, so that the schools may not turn out falsely educated men swollen with arrogance, who can hurt the Church and their own people instead of helping them." In retrospect John's attitude about public schools seems to have been less harsh than those of his predecessors. He did not consider them the ideal; but, wanting this, they were essential.[1] John allowed that the State had a duty to see that there were elementary, professional, and technical schools in rural areas. It should be observed, however, that there is a subtle distinction between "see that there are" and "establish and maintain."

In one of his most widely read statements, the encyclical *Pacem in Terris,* John XXIII wrote:

> The natural law . . . gives to man the right to share in the benefits of culture, and therefore the right to a basic education and to technical and professional training in keeping with the stage of development with the country to which he belongs. Every effort should be made to ensure that persons be enabled, on the basis of merit, to go on to higher studies, so that, as far as possible, they may occupy posts and take on responsibilities in accordance with their natural gifts and skills they have acquired.

It should be noted that John took these thoughts from the writings of his immediate predecessor, Pope Pius XII. He was simply reiterating the age-old idea of an appropriate education for all, that is, every person is entitled to an education that will best prepare him for his likely state in life. It was not a new concept with the popes, and was generally shared by the American hierarchy. Indeed, the quote could as well be attributed to Thomas Jefferson. John, however, was more liberal than his nineteenth-century precursors in defining the quantity of education that would be appropriate for all, but John did not say that everyone had the same right to an equal education.

John was a saintly man and will probably be remembered as a very great pontiff, but he was not a firebrand and not a great educational innovator. He was not against change, but he strongly approved of the time-tested methods and institutions. He called the Catholic schools "one of the Church's greatest glories." Of the parochial school system in the United States, he said: "it has borne and still bears abundant fruit . . . providing for the Church and the nation legions of fervent Catholics and exemplary citizens." John has been credited as the instigator of almost every conceivable change that has occurred in the Roman Catholic Church since 1960. His statements on education were not as copious as those of some of his predecessors though they were written in a style that was quite readable. They did not outline any radical departures from traditional "Catholic educational philosophy."

Pope John XXIII died in June, 1963 at the zenith of his popularity. His successor inherited many of the problems that were just coming to light during the Johannine years. John, as a result, did not have to contend with all of them. Ironically, John remains popular in death, but his successor is the most unpopular Pontiff in recent times. John's death was much like that of Alexander the Great, Abraham Lincoln, Franklin Roosevelt, or John Kennedy—all of whom died before they had to come to real grips with the implications of their greatest achievements. Pope John XXIII left the conclusion of the Second Vatican Council to Paul VI. Had he lived, it is very doubtful that the course of Roman Catholicism would have been appreciably different except, perhaps, that the Pontiff himself would have been more popular with the public.

It was Paul's task to carry on with the administration of the affairs of the Church after the death of Pope John. "Shortly after his election . . . Paul VI told an old friend . . . that he hoped to follow the example of his three immediate predecessors: 'Pius XI for his strong will. Pius XII for his knowledge and wisdom. John XXIII for his limitless goodness.' "[2] Paul was a liberal; but, when a pope is regarded as "liberal," it simply means that he is not opposed to change *per se*. Paul was no more in favor of abandoning Catholic traditions than was John. Of course, he was very much in favor of parochial schools. Of them, he once said:

> We recommend to you fidelity to the cause of Catholic schools. This cause must be regarded as a holy and important one in our day too, even though, unfortunately, the need and importance of it are not always acknowledged as they should be. Everyone knows of the countless difficulties that Catholic schools are facing, at the present time,

either—and this is a good thing—because of the spread of public schools, or because of the slogans of so-called statism or secularism, which are growing more or less strong everywhere.

Two things should be noted about Paul's attitude, and they actually do reflect a subtle change of tone in the thinking of much of the hierarchy. First, Paul considered the public school movement one for the good; and, second, he did not equate it with godlessness. His appraisal appears to be more realistic than that of some of his predecessors though it should be admitted, too, that the public schools have changed over the years and are now legitimately less objectionable to Roman Catholics. Paul is openly an admirer of Maria Montessori. It is unusual for a pope to comment so favorably upon a contemporary reformer, but the educational philosophy of the good Italian doctor was really quite traditional.

The greatest legacy of the Johannine Administration was the Second Vatican Council. Early in his pontificate John had announced his decision to convene Catholic leaders from around the world; on January 23, 1959, the convention was called and the first sessions began in 1962. Unlike any of the twenty previous so-called ecumenical councils, Vatican II was not called to combat a specific heresy or to deal with a specific crisis but rather to renew and update the structures of the Church. John died while the Council was in progress, and Paul VI presided over the concluding sessions. It is a matter of speculation whether the Council would have been called at all had John not been Pope. He really seemed to hurry the opening of the Council after reaching his decision to convene it. Perhaps, realizing that his death was imminent—he was almost seventy-seven when elevated to the papacy—he wanted the Council to be as far along as possible when he died so that there could be no turning back on the reforms he favored regardless of who succeeded him. Pope Pius XI and Pope Pius XII had seriously toyed with the idea of calling a Council, but, unlike Pope John XXIII, they had not considered the time propitious. In each of the tentative plans they had drawn up, there was to have been discussion of Catholic schools.

A series of documents resulted from the deliberations of Vatican II. Only one deals specifically with education though several are concerned indirectly with it. This most significant document on education is entitled the *Declaration on Christian Education*[3] and was approved by a vote of 1,588 out of 1,873 cast by the participants at the Council on November 19, 1964. Originally to have been entitled *On Catholic Schools* the document was broadened in scope and shortened in length. Revised several times, it finally was renamed *Declaration on Christian Education*. The change in the title seems to imply a recognition of the fact that Catholic education is a more encompassing concept than Catholic schools. The last draft was representative of the general consensus of opinion of the worldwide hierarchy. American bishops were in support of the document and wanted it accepted without much discussion, but many bishops from the European continent hoped that there would be a wide debate on many points. The Americans had their way because the *Declaration* was so late in being brought before the Council, just days before adjournment, that there was really not time enough left for extended deliberation. This is not to imply that the *Declaration* is a controversial document; it is not in the least.

One of the major criticisms of the document at the time it was presented was that it was too brief to treat of such a significant topic; but the *Declaration* was only intended to be descriptive, not definitive —a statement of generalities, not of particularities. Its brevity and vagueness were reasons why it was not a serious point of contention. Despite the short time allotted for discussion of the document, twenty-one participants at the Council made verbal comments on the text. Thirteen others who requested the floor were denied the opportunity to speak because of the imminent adjournment deadline. All were invited to submit their comments in writing, however; and these were received, read, and culled. A final text was then prepared, approved by the Council, and promulgated by Pope Paul VI in late 1965. There was no substantive difference between the final 1965 draft and that debated in 1964. This final copy was the eighth draft. The actual text of the *Declaration on Christian Education* was composed of an Introduction and twelve articles (1 to 4 on education in general; 5 to 7 on schools in general; 8 and 9 on Catholic schools in particular; 10 and 11 on faculties and universities; and 12 on cooperation and articulation between various Catholic schools). The document ended with a Conclusion.

The Council Fathers restated the traditional position of the

Church in favor of an appropriate education for all when they wrote that "every man . . . has an inalienable right to an education corresponding to his proper destiny and suited to his native talents, his sex, his cultural background, and his ancestral heritage." Education, they continued is a function of three societies, namely, of the family, of the State, and of the Church. Here, obviously, they were drawing from Pius XI's 1929 encyclical *Divini illius Magistri*. The family, the bishops agreed, was the primary educator. While not yielding an iota of the Church's rights as regarded education, the *Declaration* was concerned first with the rights of the State and then of the Church. Perhaps this was an unintentional stylistic device, but it does obviate some of the harshness that was in the letter of Pope Pius XI, and its position on public schools is not so negative. "While belonging primarily to the family," reads the *Declaration*,

> the task of imparting education requires the help of society as a whole. In addition, therefore, to the rights of parents and of others to whom parents entrust a share in the work of education, certain rights and duties belong to civil society. For this society exists to arrange for the temporal necessities of the common good. Part of its duty is to promote the education of the young in several ways: namely, by overseeing the duties and rights of parents and of others who have a role in education, and by providing them with assistance; by implementing the principle of subsidiarity and by completing the task of education, with the attention to parental wishes, whenever the efforts of parents and other groups are insufficient; and, moreover, by building its own schools and institutes as the common good may demand.

But, all things considered, the *Declaration on Christian Education* states very little about public schools.

There was divided opinion at the Council concerning the wisdom of inserting some sort of paragraph supporting public aid for Catholic schools. Cardinal Spellman strongly favored a clause as did many American prelates. The compromise statement read as follows:

> The state itself ought to protect the right of children to receive an adequate schooling. It should be vigilant about the ability of teachers and the excellence of their training. It should look after the health of students and, in general promote the whole school enterprise. But it must keep in mind the principle of subsidiarity, so that no kind of school monopoly arises.

The *Declaration* gives unequivocal support to the principle of "subsidiarity" as a guiding policy in education. This principle was defined as follows in the *Pastoral Constitution of the Church in the Modern World,* another of the Vatican II documents:

> The principle of subsidiarity formulated by Pope Pius XI in the encyclical letter "Quadragesimo Anno" reads: 'This supremely important principle of social philosophy, one which cannot be set aside or altered, remains firm and unshaken: Just as it is wrong to withdraw from the individual and commit to the community at large what private enterprise and endeavor can accomplish, so it is likewise unjust and a gravely harmful disturbance of right order to turn over to a greater society of higher rank functions and services which can be performed by lesser bodies on a lower plane. For a social undertaking of any sort, by its very nature, ought to aid the members of the body social, but never to destroy or absorb them.'[4]

Governments at the state and local level, it would seem from this, are to aid private schools so that they do not have to price themselves out of existence. Any undesirable "school monopoly" would be a situation where there would be only public schools. The Church Fathers apparently did not see their endorsement of subsidiarity as inconsistent with the declaration of support of public assistance for church-related schools. It would seem, however, that the state or federal governments would each be a "greater society of higher rank" than the individual private families in any given parish. Subsidiarity is a dangerous argument. The pivotal question rests with the word "can." If the family "can," then the state should not. If the state "can," then the federal government should not. The Roman Catholic parochial schools in the United States today are in grave financial difficulty. Some Catholics argue that Catholic families "can" no longer afford the schools and that, according to the principle of subsidiarity, the government should now step forward with assistance. These proponents of government aid ask their fellow citizens to believe that present-day Catholics cannot do what their immigrant forebears were able to do, namely, foster an independent school system. If Catholics "can" but simply "will" not pay the costs of a separate school system, then the *Declaration on Christian Education* itself, drawing on a long series of traditional writings, condemns plans for state aid.

Vatican Council II participants formally acknowledged the special obligation of the Church to children not enrolled in Catholic schools. This was one of the more original parts of the *Declaration,* and it has some application to American Catholic youngsters who are not attending parochial schools, but most bishops probably had other countries in mind where there are virtually no Catholic schools at all. American bishops, reflecting the commitment to parish schools in the United States, would undoubtedly have liked to have seen much more specific discussion regarding parochial schools. In another original section of the document the bishops approved of permitting non-Catholic children to attend Catholic schools. This had long been practiced in the Church in various places but had never received such significant, explicit approval from Rome. Catholic schools, concluded the Fathers, may rightly vary with local circumstances, and "thus the Church feels a most cordial esteem for those Catholic schools, found especially where the Church is newly established, which contain large numbers of non-Catholic students." Such concern for those not of the faith has not often been officially expressed in such an important pronouncement. Another of the more interesting statements on education made in the Vatican documents is that all Catholic school teachers should meet regular state certification standards.

Catholic as well as non-Catholic schools share certain cultural goals and certain developmental goals dictated by the physical nature of children; but Catholic schools, asserted the Council Fathers, have certain unique purposes. Catholic schools seek to create an atmosphere of genuine freedom and charity. They seek to develop the physical personality of the child in consonance with his spiritual growth, and they seek to relate all human culture to the news of salvation. Really, what the Council participants were saying here was little different from what Pope Pius XI had said in *Divini illius Magistri* when he wrote that the total curriculum should be permeated with Roman Catholic piety.[5] Touching upon yet another issue treated by Pope Pius XI, the *Declaration* stated that children "as they advance in years . . . should receive prudent sexual education." Once again this was not really different from the traditional position; but it was stated in such a way that it lent itself to broad interpretation.

Other Council documents are concerned with education but only in an indirect way. For instance, *The Decree on the Bishops' Pastoral Office in the Church* reaffirms the canonical fact that Catholic schools that are run by non-diocesan priests, nuns, and brothers are subject to the local bishops as regards matters of general policy and supervision through their actual direction rests in the hands of the religious themselves. This was somewhat new in the United States where previously the bishop's control was absolute only over diocesan schools. This article does not confer unfettered authority upon the bishop, but it does appear to broaden his power on paper at least. It is doubtful whether this change will have any significant effect. The movement toward centralization of Catholic educational facilities within each diocese was underway before the Council. Some feel that an ultimate effect of the *Decree on the Appropriate Renewal of Religious Life* might be that religious brothers and sisters will no longer be assigned to teach before they have met the same standards required of public school teachers. This is consonant with the desire expressed in the *Declaration on Christian Education* that Catholic school teachers meet regular certification requirements. Increasing state vigilance over private schools will unintentionally fulfill this Council suggestion.

Not all persons would agree in their interpretation of the Council writings as regards education. Many would agree that they mark a "bold change in direction for the Church."[6] Others are less convinced of the significance of these documents.[7] Some feel that what change has come about in Catholic thinking on education predates Vatican II.[8] There is no doubt about it, the official tone has changed; but there is not such certainty that basic fundamental positions have been altered. The Roman Catholic Church, as an institution which claims for itself an infallible magisterium in matters of faith and morals, is very much like the Supreme Court of the United States. The teachings of the Church are based largely on the "errorless" interpretations of a body of revealed truths and longstanding traditions. These interpretations are like the decisions of the High Court. It is extremely difficult to get a complete reversal when a ruling has once been handed down. In the Church, such a turn-around would not only have political repercussions: it would also have grave theological implications. While it is true that none of the educational writings of the popes have been *ex cathedra,* that is, infallible definitions on faith or morals, they have come to be viewed as highly authoritative because of the cloak of the infallibility that is believed to fall upon the shoulders of the man who holds the office of Supreme Pontiff. They have been accepted at face value throughout the Church virtually without debate.

The *Declaration on Christian Education* is really a very traditional statement. It had to be such a document not because the Roman Catholic Church is incapable of taking a bold position but rather because it must always take a consistent position if it is to maintain its authority. It cannot admit to having made serious errors. Had the *Declaration* been a revolutionary document, it would not have been approved with so little real debate by a convention of the guardians of Roman Catholic orthodoxy. There are fifty-five footnote citations in the *Declaration,* and they give silent testimony on the bottom of every page to its conservative origin. The majority of these references are to papal writings: nine to statements by Pope Paul VI, twelve to John XXIII, fourteen to Pius XII, sixteen to Pius XI, and one to Benedict XV. Of the sixteen references to the works of Pope Pius XI who is quoted more than any other pope, twelve are to the *Divini illius Magistri.* The 1929 encyclical of Pope Pius XI was apparently the most influential single document in the drafting of the *Declaration on Christian Education.* Indeed even its Anglicized title, "Christian Education of Youth," is very similar to that of the Council document. Both emphasize the rights and duties of parents, the State, and the Church. The Vatican II document is less pedantic than the encyclical. It describes but does not define education. It takes a position that is more open to the world at large. It displays less suspicion toward public education. Still the *Declaration* "breaks little new ground" and "the Church has not changed its traditional positions."[9]

The Council document on education is often quoted in Catholic circles, and there have been many changes in Catholic education since the Declaration was promulgated, but it does not necessarily follow that the latter is related to the former as cause is to effect. Like the decrees of Baltimore III, those of Vatican II on education will no doubt be seen by many as the source of the great changes that are going on in the parochial school system. It seems more probable, however, that the spirit which caused, even forced, the convocation of the Ecumenical Council is really what is bringing about these changes in Catholic education and not any specific utterances of the Catholic bishops. The history of the parochial school system in America would seem to indicate that individual official pronouncements have little real influence on the future course of development of the system. This has been true of the various pastorals and of the papal encyclicals. What changes that have occurred have been caused by other factors, such as the improving socioeconomic status of the typical Catholic, the "Americanization" of the Catholic immigrant, increasing state involvement in education, the growing influence of voluntary accrediting agencies, the changing nature of the American public school, growing public interest in education, and the growth of education as a highly technical field. However, Catholics have sometimes failed to realize this. Perhaps this, too, will be the fate of the *Declaration on Christian Education*. Perhaps it will become a means by which the changes in the school system can be rationalized.

There have been many changes in the Catholic parochial school system that have occurred concomitantly with Vatican II. The most significant of these has been a declining number of school units and falling enrollments. As early as the late fifties there was a relative decrease in school enrollments though some Church leaders may have failed to see it as it was masked in an absolute increase in numbers. Since the middle sixties the number of children enrolled in Catholic schools has decreased in absolute as well as relative figures. By 1970 the number of schools and the size of enrollments had fallen to the levels of the late fifties. This decline was the largest recorded in the history of the system. It was just one facet of an overall crisis in the American Catholic Church which in 1970 recorded an actual loss in the number of its adherents.[10]

Why have enrollments declined so precipitously? This is the contemporary American Catholic's version of the riddle of the Sphinx. Many Catholic parents are quite obviously not so convinced as they once were that the parochial schools are necessary or desirable or better than public schooling or worth the financial sacrifices. As a result the schools are in grave financial difficulty, and many Catholic educators have come to view the money squeeze as the most serious contemporary problem. Articles on school finance and on public aid programs fill the pages of religious publications and of Catholic educational journals. Church leaders have become increasingly active in their demands for public support for private schools. Whereas in the late thirties, the forties, the fifties, their arguments were couched in abstract terms of social justice, in the sixties their approach became more legalistic. They began to adopt the tactics of the lawyer and the professional lobbyist. Still the Roman Catholic hierarchy has never consulted the rank and file of the laity as to their position on the question of government aid. Parents of children in parochial schools are more in support of state aid than parents of youngsters in public schools; but Catholic parents are not so adamant in their support as one might at first expect.[11] As more Catholic parents remove their children from the parochial schools, they will become parents of children in public schools. Catholics are getting out of the parochial school habit. As this continues to occur, it would seem a safe conclusion to say that the American hierarchy will find it harder, not easier, to muster support for their lobby positions.

The financial squeeze has several causes: increasing hardware and software in the classroom; increasing demands for fully trained professional teachers; decreasing numbers of religious personnel; and inflation. The fact remains, however, that the school system was erected by immigrants less well-to-do than present-day Catholics. They built the schools and supported them because they felt they were worth their material sacrifices. Contemporary Catholics apparently do not. The distinction is an important one because it reveals the fact that the financial crisis in the Catholic schools is not the most serious problem but rather a symptom of the most serious problem, namely, dwindling commitment to the concept of parochial schools. Government funds will only relieve the outward signs of the growing crisis. Government doles will not muster lay Catholic support. They will not bring about an increase in religious vocations. They will not persuade those who have left to return to their convents and rectories. The real problem is one of faith, not of finances. Public assistance might make the situation better for a while, but in the long run it could be ruinous. One of the necessary concomitants of goverment aid is public regulation. The more state supervision, the more Catholic schools will become like public schools. The more that parochial schools appear to be carbon copies of state institutions, the less Catholics will see the need to do without to support them. As Bishop John Carroll noted 170 years ago, the ultimate success of the Catholic schools rests upon the support of the faithful.

There are, no doubt, some Catholic parents who cannot afford the tuition of parochial schools. Some, too, are uneasy about the unsettling changes occuring in contemporary Catholicism. Some equate Catholic education with nuns and cannot see any reason to pay to send their children to a parochial school where they will be taught by lay persons. For many years the typical Catholic was quite ignorant of what went on in the public schools. His picture of the neighborhood school was very much like the portrait Maria Monk painted of the Montreal convent where she was supposedly a prisoner. As more and more parents put their children into public schools, however, Catholics in general are becoming more realistic in their concept of the public schools. The "Americanization" of Catholics is just about completed. The typical Catholic is not very different from any other American. Most have lost the ethnic subculture that the Catholic schools were founded to protect and preserve. These are some of the factors which explain falling enrollment figures. Lower attendance numbers, of course, account for some of the decline in the number of Catholic school units though another explanatory factor is a shift in the Catholic population. Since the middle of the first half of the nineteenth century, Catholics have been predominantly urban dwellers in this country, but since World War II they have become metropolitan, moving out from the inner city to the periphery and suburbs. Some large city parishes have fewer parishioners than they did years ago and cannot now support large schools.

To meet these crises, some dioceses have had to cut back on school spending. The Diocese of Rochester and the Archdiocese of Saint Louis, for instance, have put a moratorium on school building. The Archdiocese of Cincinnati has done likewise and has also eliminated grades one through four. In the Dioceses of Saginaw, Spokane, Kansas City, Fargo, Richmond, and Green Bay certain grades have been eliminated. Very few parishes now maintain their own kindergarten; and the end to forced retrenchment programs appears to be nowhere in sight.

Unsurprisingly, the Catholic school system has come to be the subject of much criticism. More and more writings on Catholic education are being published every year, and articles questioning the need and even the desirability of the system not infrequently appear in Church publications—something that was virtually unheard of before 1960. One of the more significant of these was Mary Perkins Ryan's lengthy essay *Are Parochial Schools the Answer? Catholic Education in the Light of the Council.*[12] Her treatment was widely read and caused such a furor that forty thousand dollars was funded at the 1964 National Catholic Educational Association convention for a rebuttal that would tell the success story of the Catholic schools.[13] Mrs. Ryan's treatment was a position paper that reflected her faith more than her scholarship. One might almost consider her treatment a liturgical interpretation of Catholic education. She summarized her own arguments in these words:

> In the context of the new outlook [namely, of Vatican II], two major conclusions would seem to be inevitable: first, that a truly Catholic formation for all young people is a real possibility if we use all the resources at our disposal; and second, that a general education under Catholic auspices is no longer as necessary or even as desirable as in the past. As things are, the maintenance of our Catholic school system —not to speak of its extension—takes up a large part of our available human resources, resources now needed for urgent religious tasks. Even if some form of public aid were to relieve us of part of the financial burden, should we then plan for continued maintenance of our Catholic school system in the future.

Mrs. Ryan also stated that she saw three possible courses of future action: (1) to maintain the school system as has been the practice for at least the past ninety years which, according to her interpretation, would not be strictly in keeping with the aims of Vatican II; (2) to obtain public support or set up some sort of shared-time programs, but these, she felt, would deflect vital manpower from vital ecumenical works; or (3) to chart out bold new courses and concentrate on renewal. Ryan's contentions were rather typical of some of those advanced by the more *avant garde* of the clergy and laity. They did not represent the opinion of the majority of the laity or clergy, and certainly not of the hierarchy. Ryan's interpretation of the Vatican documents is subject to question. Unfortunately, she suffers from a syndrome not uncommon in persons pulling a bandwagon: she has a hard time appreciating merit in any other causes but her own.

Mrs. Ryan has not been an isolated critic. Many have been impressed by the Greeley and Rossi study of Catholic parochial schools and draw from it quasi-scientific support for some of their arguments. One of the most significant findings of Greeley and Rossi was that "there is no evidence that Catholic schools have been necessary for the survival of American Catholicism." It is interesting to note that, writing in the mid-sixties, they failed to see the imminent enrollment crisis and stated that ". . . Catholic education has never been more popular. Truly the demand seems to be at an all-time high and is likely to increase with the increase in social class appearing among American Catholics."[14] Certainly the Greeley and Rossi report is not the last word on the subject. Some Roman Catholics who disagree might recall the sermon of Bernard McQuaid at Baltimore III in 1884 with alarm. "Without these schools," warned Bishop McQuaid, "in a few generations our magnificent cathedrals and churches would remain as samples of monumental folly—of the unwisdom of a capitalist who consumes his fortune year by year without putting it out at interest or allowing it to increase." Other arguments pointing to the shortcomings of the schools besides their being nonessential are that they create a ghetto mentality among Catholics, that they are socially divisive, that they fail to produce a proportionate number of intellectuals, that they overstress athletics, that they understress athletics, that they do not turn out youngsters adequately prepared to earn a living, that there is too much emphasis on religion, that there is no longer enough emphasis on religion, that they concentrate too much of the Church's resources on elementary education, that they confuse the pastoral for the academic, that they are dominated by the clergy, that one school per parish is wasteful and inefficient, and that the teachers that staff them are inadequately prepared.

The American hierarchy, to say the least, has been gravely concerned about the increasingly obvious school crisis; but one gets the distinct impression that many of them are bewildered by it. The problem is not uniform throughout the country, and so any definitive, blanket, national pronouncement is precluded. The Roman Catholic school system, if viewed from the standpoint of being a gigantic business, is unique in that ultimate direction is in the hands of nonprofessionals. The bishops—most of whom have had a classical education, many of whom have had their seminary training in Rome, few of whom are certified and experienced classroom teachers, principals or superintendents—have the final authority though other persons may have the titles of superintendent, principal, or school board member. In actual practice the American hierarchy has never really seemed to have been completely willing to view education as a truly specialized and separate discipline. Individual bishops have constantly intervened in matters of educational policy that have been quite remote from faith and morals. One suspects that they would not do this in a Catholic hospital or in a Catholic professional school. This tendency has not created the current school problem but it has, on occasion, made it worse or prevented remedies from being taken that would somewhat meliorate the situation, for example, a bishop may decide to split a parish in two and build a second school even though the original attendance district was inadequate to support one school. By its very nature, the parochial school system forces certain educational issues to be religious issues also and *vice versa*. One of the difficulties that would be encountered in any large-scale public aid program would be that the educational and the religious would have to be clearly delineated if not separated. The problem is really just a variation of the question of "permeation" of the curriculum with the religious element which Pope Pius XI considered a principal justification for the existence of the parochial school system.

Acting through the National Committee of Bishops, the American hierarchy issued a statement on the parochial school crisis in 1967.[15] Though short, it was the most specific statement of the bishops on the question in the decade. They promised, too, a lengthy pastoral devoted exclusively to the topic at some future time. Their letter, not surprisingly, set forth no basic departures from traditional teachings or practice. It had a tone somewhat akin to the pep talk a coach might deliver to a ball team. The bishops stressed the financial burdens of the schools, but they strongly reaffirmed their commitment to parochial schools though candidly admitting that some mistakes might have been made in the past. "There is no point," they wrote, "in criticizing the past for not having the vision of the present." They quoted some of the Vatican II documents. They also reaffirmed the worthiness of teaching as an aspostolate, and this is a most interesting part of their statement. It seems to be directed to those religious leaving the classrooms. Many priests and brothers and nuns are entering into the lay life, but many are merely leaving the classrooms and opting for some other type of full-time occupation. Though statistics are still incomplete, it does seem a safe generalization to make that among those remaining in the convents and rectories classroom teaching does not seem so popular or so prestigious as it once was. The 1967 statement of the American hierarchy suggested no clear-cut solutions for the current crisis but instead it appeared to assure the rank and file that the hierarchy was aware of the present situation and that it was not about to abandon the cause of parochial education.

Just as it is hazardous to make safe generalizations about the entire parochial school system, it is difficult but necessary to make some predictions about its future. Tomorrow's system will be considerably smaller in size. It will probably be of a higher quality than has often been the case in the past. It will become more of a private school system as the unattainable and maybe dubious ideal of "every Catholic child in a Catholic school" is abandoned. The system will become more homogeneous within each diocese as the chancery comes to exercise more and more control. The clergy will play a lesser role, and the laity a greater one, but though clerical domination may be dying it is hardly dead yet. There will be greater professionalism among parochial school teachers, and there will also be increasing organization for collective bargaining among them. Government aid will probably not be forthcoming on the scale that some would hope, and tuitions will rise to a point that will make the parochial schools a system for the elite. One of the distinguishing characteristics of the parochial school system in the United States heretofore has been that it was a private school system that was within the financial grasp of the masses, but this hallmark will largely disappear in the future. The decline in enrollments and in the number of school units will continue, and the would-be Catholic school students will be absorbed by the public schools. If there is any kind of cleavage in the Roman Church in the United States between high-church and low-church elements caused by the current reform movements, the more conservative high-church factions will probably support schools more than the more nontraditional wing. Parochial schools will not disappear altogether. As an educational entity they have existed since the Middle Ages, and it is hard to envision something that has existed for one thousand years vanishing completely in just one generation.

* * *

The period of American Catholic history spanning the years 1958 to the present might be viewed as the beginning of an epoch labelled the "Era of the Americans." Some might disagree with the choice of title and argue instead that it should be called the "Ecumenical Era." Strong arguments can be raised for either selection. However, to call the last decade the "Ecumenical Era" would seem to imply that most of the changes in the American Church, more particularly in the schools, were caused chiefly by the Second Vatican Council. Many of these changes, however, had their real roots in events that occurred before the accession of Pope John XXIII. It must be admitted, however, that the ecumenism often associated with John has tended to blunt the traditional "defense of the faith" mentality in Catholic education. As for the school system, it really never fully recovered from the decline during the Depression. Indeed the actual percentage of Catholic children in Catholic schools never again reached pre-Depression year heights. The period of time in question is unique in American Catholic Church history because it has been marked by no significant mass Catholic immigration. The majority of American Catholics are now natural-born citizens, and the typical Catholic child today has natural-born parents. It is probably safe to say that the decline of the school system is due more to the immigration restriction quotas set in the nineteen-twenties than to any council or hierarchical writings. The Catholic ghetto has largely disappeared. Official writings of the Church now appear to be directed more to the explaining of contemporary changes rather than to the mapping out of markedly new programs. It is one of the ironies of history that the Catholic parochial school system may be "dying" because of its own success. It was originally intended, among other things, to guide the process of "Americanization." That process is completed. The Church is no longer a church of immigrants. It is made up of Americans, hence the "Era of the Americans."

And so one comes to the present. The American Catholic parochial school system is and remains for the time being the largest privately established network of schools in the history of the world—a living monument to the immigrants who built it at the cost of much personal sacrifice despite opposition both from within and without the Church. These are days of change and uncertainty. What will really happen to these schools is yet to be seen. Orestes Brownson observed 109 years ago that the parochial school "movement, has, wisely or unwisely, been set on foot, and gone too far to be arrested, even if it were desirable to arrest it." He was right; and what he said is, no doubt, still true.

NOTES

1. John XXIII, *Encyclical Mater et Magistra,* May 15, 1961, in *Seven Great Encyclicals,* p. 246.
2. "Religion: The Path to Follow," *Time* (June 28, 1963), pp. 40–47, quote from p. 47.
3. The text appears in Walter M. Abbott (general ed.), *The Documents of Vatican II* (New York: Guild Press, America Press, Association Press, 1966), pp. 637–651. All future references to the document are based on this text.
4. "The Pastoral Constitution of the Church in the Modern World," in Abbott, p. 300n.
5. The *Declaration* rejects the possibility "of making a clear distinction between the sacral and the secular," notes Monsignor O'Neil D'Amour "Vatican II on Christian Education," *Ave Maria,* Volume CIV, Number 20 (November 12, 1966), pp. 20–22.
6. For example: D'Amour, p. 20. Justin A. Driscoll, "A Philosophy of Catholic Education in a Time of Change . . . ," *The Catholic School Journal,* Volume LXVII, Number 9 (November, 1967), pp. 29–33.
7. "We must honestly admit that the Council's influence on the discussion of Catholic schools has not come from its Constitution on Christian Education." John L. Reedy and James F. Andrews, "Catholic Schools—Searching for the Total View," *Ave Maria,* Volume CIV, Number 16 (1966), p. 19.
8. For example: Roy J. Deferrari, *A Complete System of Catholic Education Is Necessary: A Reply to "Are Parochial Schools the Answer?" by Mary Perkins Ryan* (Boston: Saint Paul Editions, Daughters of Saint Paul, 1964), p. 145. George Shuster put this point across amusingly when he wrote: "The author [viz., Shuster] will appear stubbornly unimpressed with the notion that the world began when Vatican II ended." *Catholic Education in a Changing World,* p. ix.
9. G. Emmett Carter, "Introduction," in Abbott, pp. 634–636. Herbert Vorgrimler (ed.), *Commentary on the Documents of Vatican II,* Volume IV (West Germany: Herder and Herder, 1969). Mark J. Hurley, "The Declaration on Christian Education," *The Homiletic and Pastoral Review,* Volume LXVI (December, 1965), pp. 224–227.

    D'Amour seems to argue that the document was drawn from the American milieu more than from Europe's; and, if this is indeed true, then the document is truly unique. He writes that "the principles that form the background for the Declaration are drawn more from Dr. John Dewey, Monsignor George Johnson, and Sister Mary Nona than from the writings of Pope Pius XI or Thomas Aquinas," p. 21. It seems to this writer that D'Amour, like so many contemporary Catholic educators, is reading more into the document than is actually written there.
10. According to an article in *U.S. News and World Report,* the enrollment in Catholic grade schools and high schools in 1963 was 5,590,806; and in 1969, an estimated 4,820,000—or a decrease in six years of 770,806 pupils. According to the same report, in 1963 there were 13,205 schools; and in 1969, an estimated 12,182—or a decrease of 1,023. According to the *Catholic Directory* the peak year for the system in terms of size was 1965 when there were 4,476,881 youngsters in 10,563 elementary schools. "Crisis Hits Catholic Schools," *U.S. News and World Report* (September 29, 1969), pp. 33–34. For the *Directory* statistics, see the tables in the Appendix. According to the *Catholic Directory,* there were 47,872,089 Roman Catholics in the United States in 1970 as opposed to 47,873,268 in 1969 or a loss of 1,179.
11. George Gallup, "Second Annual Survey of the Public's Attitude toward the

NOTES

Public Schools," *Phi Delta Kappan,* Volume LII, Number 2 (October, 1970), p. 103.
12. Ryan (Chicago: Holt, Rinehart and Winston, 1964).
13. A final product was Defarrari's essay. It really failed to counter Ryan's arguments adequately. For instance, Defarrari faulted Ryan for failure to rely on appropriate source materials (p. 41), and yet his own essay contained only four footnotes and no bibliography.
14. Greeley and Rossi, pp. 225, 236.
15. National Conference of U.S. Catholic Bishops, "Statement by U.S. Bishops on Catholic Schools (November 16, 1967)," *Catholic Mind,* Volume LXVI, No. 1219 (January, 1968), pp. 1–6.

VI
Epilogue

Parochial schools are not an educational phenomenon unique to the Roman Catholic Church or to the Church in the United States. Parish schools, as instruments of formal education, predate the Middle Ages, and many Christian denominations have supported them at various times and in various places. Roman Catholic parochial schools did not exist in America during the colonial period, but they became widespread during the early national period. It was only after the Civil War, however, in the later decades of the nineteenth century that these schools became sufficiently numerous and well enough organized to be referred to as a "system."

Though parochial schools are not unique, the American Catholic school system is one of a kind. It is the largest private school system in the world and in the history of western civilization. Though maintained largely through the voluntary contributions of Roman Catholics, it provides education for the masses. Most private school systems are tailored to the needs of an elite, but the Catholic school system has been atypical.

There were many reasons why American Catholics came to support parish schools. Parochial schools were seen by many as a means of preserving ethnicity, of perpetuating the customs and values and language of the Old World heritage. To many of the immigrants these schools offered a way in which the subculture and ways of the Old Country could be handed down intact to their children. At the same time, many saw in the parochial schools an entirely different purpose, namely, to provide a controlled means of "Americanization." Some argued that the schools were the ideal instruments by which immigrant children could be introduced into the American culture since the environment would be superintended by the Church. "Americanization," however, was defined differently by different groups. One side contended that the other was so anxious to be accepted by the mainstream of American society that it was willing to compromise fundamentals of the faith. The counterargument was raised, however, that some groups within the Church were so reluctant to discard the old ways that they were really second-class citizens.

The parochial school movement paralleled in many ways the common school movement. Like the public schools, there was a tremendous growth in the number of school units continuing from the first half of the nineteenth century. There was also a trend after the Civil War to organize the schools into administrative units. Other parallels can be seen in the growing percentage of women behind the desks in the front of the classrooms; the schoolmarms had their counterparts in the nuns. In the Catholic schools, as in the common schools, education was tending to become more of a science. Better textbooks, improved equipment, teachers with superior professional training, and the application of more modern theories of learning—all these things and others, to varying degrees—were found in Catholic as well as public schools as the nineteenth century blended into the twentieth.

The idea that everyone should receive some sort of formal schooling was becoming generally accepted, and the common-school movement indirectly encouraged the building of Catholic parochial schools. Originally, the public schools tended to be quite anti-Catholic. Later they were more nondenominational Protestant in nature. Today it would probably be safe to say that most public schools are nonsectarian. Many Catholics still harbor a traditional distrust of public schools as Catholic schools were long seen as the only acceptable means to provide Catholic children with the necessary and legally required education. Of course many also felt, and many still do feel, that Catholic schools were, and are, essential to preserve the faith of Roman Catholic youngsters against serious dangers posed by a predominantly Protestant, if not hostile, society. By the late 1870's the Vatican authorities, aroused by the dire predictions and warnings submitted by non-English-speaking groups in the United States, had become convinced that parochial schools must be made mandatory if the Church was to survive in America.

Several of the original motives for building Catholic schools no longer exist. The original subcultures which the schools were designed to protect have largely disappeared. The public schools are generally unobjectionable, and Catholics are becoming increasingly aware of this. The fact that Catholics so long held themselves aloof from the public schools inculcated much ignorance within Catholic circles as to what the common schools were really like. Many Roman Catholics, educated and reared entirely within the Catholic ghetto, had no firsthand experience with public schools and have often entertained notions of them that would have been truer of schools of generations earlier. One still hears Catholics occasionally refer to the fabulous wealth of the public elementary school systems, or to the enormous salaries paid to public school employees, or to the elaborate equipment which is in every state school. One Catholic school principal who was having difficulties with her school board recently threatened to resign remarking that in the public schools in the area her salary would be at least thirty thousand dollars a year. Another manifestation of this syndrome is the comment heard now and again from Catholics about the terrible disciplinary problems that are supposedly the rule rather than the exception in public schools. As more and more Catholics attend public schools with each passing year, they realize that these schools do not pose this kind of threat and that the differences between Catholic and public schools are not so great as often imagined. The immigrants are gone, and their descendants are Americans, and the public schools have changed.

Faith and papal encouragement still are motives for support of the schools, but at the present time they do not seem sufficiently strong to maintain an adequate grass roots base for the schools. Changes in the liturgy and apparent shifts in the traditional teachings of the Church tend to weaken the motive of preservation of the faith in the minds of many Catholics. It seems to some that the faith is changing. The exodus of priests and nuns from the rectories and convents and their public defiance of religious authorities points to a weakening influence of official directives. There is an authority crisis in the Church as well as a crisis in the faith.

Though few foresaw it a decade ago, the Catholic schools have undergone a significant decline in number and in membership in recent years. This decrease in number was preceded for at least thirty years by a relative decrease in the percentage of Catholic youngsters attending Catholic schools. This relative decline, however, was masked by the fact that there was an absolute rise in the number of parochial school units and in attendance statistics. Those few who observed the dichotomy between the two sets of figures were dismissed as Cassandras. Not surprisingly, many Roman Catholic educators have renewed and increased their lobby efforts in behalf of public aid for private schools. The degree of pressure applied by churchmen in this area is unprecedented. Both proponents and opponents of public aid programs cite the first amendment to the federal Constitution in behalf of their position. The recent history of the Supreme Court would seem to demonstrate the futility of predicting what final dispositions will be made on this or on any other issue. If the Court rules government aid illegal, all arguments become moot; if the Court finds it constitutional, many rationales can be made in attempts to persuade federal and state legislatures to appropriate and earmark funds.

One very powerful argument that is commonly brought up is that the present situation puts the burden of "double taxation" upon the parents of a child in a Catholic school; school taxes are paid and tuition payments are made. Historically, this is probably the oldest pro-aid argument, and it has been raised time and again over the past century. There are some proponents who take a more pragmatic stance and argue that aid will be less expensive in the long run because Catholic schools will close without public funds and it will then cost more to absorb youngsters into public schools than to maintain existing private schools. One of the most powerful arguments raised for aid is that the Catholic schools are a significant part of the American educational heritage and that without substantial financial support they will go out of existence. Those adopting this position often point out that Catholic schools, where they are strong, provide a real service to American education by offering a viable alternative to public schools. One other variation of the argument raised in behalf of public funding is that of "subsidiarity." This position is to the effect that schools should be supported at the simplest level. Proponents of aid to church-related schools often interpret this to mean that Catholic schools should receive state aid but not federal aid. Despite the fact that this position had had the endorsement of the hierarchy over the past fifty years, it is a treacherous argument. The lowest support base is the parent paying tuition and not the state appropriating funds. Aid proponents who talk of subsidiarity lay the grounds for arguments by which they can be refuted. All proponents of public aid operate under the basic assumption that more money will remedy the woes of today's Catholic schools.

There is no doubt about the fact that Catholic schools are experiencing a real shortage of funds, but the financial difficulty is merely the symptom of what is really ailing the Catholic schools. Lack of money is not the problem, rather it is a lack of conviction on the part of contemporary Catholics that the schools are desirable or better than public schools or worth the added sacrifice it would take to patronize and maintain them. It is hard to believe that a system that was built by immigrants cannot be supported by their children and their grandchildren. It seems more accurate to say Catholics are no longer willing to support the schools rather than to say that they are no longer able to support them. And hence the whole problem is really more than a mere educational one. The lack of funds reflects a diminishing commitment to the concept of parochial schools as does the declining number of persons living in religious teaching communities. Many rationales can be raised to justify public financial assistance, but will more money really work? Will the nuns return to the classroom? Will the enrollments rise? Will the rank and file once again display the same degree of confidence in the value and efficacy of parochial schools? Can money infuse the system with a new sense of purpose?

If a new sense of purpose cannot be provided by money, will it be likely to come from the official leadership in the Church? If one can judge from the past and from the official pronouncements relating to Catholic education and to parochial schools, the answer would appear to be "no." Official writings do not seem to have been as significant as other factors in explaining the rise of the system. Ethnicity seems to have been a more important factor. The writings of the popes and of the hierarchy were more often descriptions of existing situations than prescriptions for bold new programs. They reflected little of the internal struggles over the school issue. A mere reading of these documents does not present a very complete picture of the history of the Catholic parochial school movement. Papal documents seem to have been less significant than the statements of the American hierarchy, especially before 1870. Papal documents have become increasingly numerous during the past one hundred years. Whereas American bishops have always paid lip service to papal missives, they have not always been able to carry them out fully. Papal letters often seemed more geared to the milieu on the European continent than in the United States of America. The general procedures by which the Church leadership is chosen make firebrands like John Ireland the exception rather than the rule.

Although it is not easy to make predictions about the future, it would probably be safe to say that the numbers of Catholic parochial schools and their enrollments will decline substantially in the future but will not totally disappear. It would be very unlikely that the Church would officially and totally abandon her commitment to the concept of parish schools. It would not fit the historical pattern, moreover, if the official documents of the future outlined radical departures from traditional Catholic practices and mapped out entirely new courses of action. Any such occurrences will come from other sources. Admittedly it is easy to make suggestions for future policy, difficult to implement them. Certainly money will help to alleviate the current problems of the Catholic schools, but it will definitely not remove them. What assistance programs can do at best is provide time in which an attempt might be made to reconstruct commitment on the part of the man-in-the-pew to the concept of parochial schools. New motives for support of the schools must be sought. The most obvious of these is to make parish schools models of educational excellence that will provide a viable alternative to public school education. One advantage private education has over public schools is that it can be freer to innovate, and it is time Catholic school administrators start to cash in on this fully. The existing motives for supporting parochial education must be conserved and strengthened. The religious element in the schools must be kept strong, not de-emphasized. The great questions of life—who am I?; why am I here?; where, if anywhere, am I going?—have many answers. The public schools, in an attempt to be unbiased, have often not only avoided giving any particular answer but have also eliminated these questions entirely from the curriculum. Private schools can ask these questions and can endorse specific solutions. Religious education is a product that may still have a substantial potential market. It is interesting to note that as more and more changes have occurred within the Church, school attendance and support have declined. Though it is not possible to equate the exact relationship between these factors, perhaps it does suggest that Catholic educators should take a more traditional, even conservative stance in their approach to religion. It was, after all, the pre-Counciliar Catholic who supported the schools and the old "unemancipated" nun who sat behind the desks in its classrooms. Perhaps what all of this indicates is that the schools should be symbols of religious orthodoxy and of stability in a period of history in which basic values and traditions are being strongly challenged. To preserve the faith can still be a powerful purpose for supporting parochial education. Priests and nuns, too, must be willing to support the schools by their own public activities. Official directives in support of the schools ring hollow when clergymen publicly question the desirability of parochial education and when many nuns prefer to abandon the classroom to pursue more "relevant" apostolates.

The possible topics for future research in the area of Catholic parochial education are many. There is a need for a well-documented compilation of the primary sources pertaining to the history of the schools. Existing anthologies are incomplete and dated by events occurring since their publication. The influence of some of the more dominant personalities in the history of American Catholicism on Catholic education itself needs to be explored. Starts in this direction have been made but more needs to be done. Comparative studies between Catholic parochial schools in the United States and in other countries would be of value as would be comparative studies of Catholic and non-Catholic schools. In a more sociological vein, it would be interesting to attempt to determine what motives present-day Catholics have when they remove or decide not to enroll their children in parochial schools. More than anything else this might give a gauge of future enrollments.

The past history of the schools has been colorful; the present, marked by many significant developments; and it does not appear that the future will be any less eventful.

Appendix

CHRONOLOGICAL SUMMARY

- 1634 Maryland established by English Catholics. Spanish, French, and German Catholics also engaged in educational activities in other parts of America throughout the colonial period.
- 1780–1850 Trustee controversy.
- 1789 John Carroll becomes first bishop of Baltimore.
- 1800–1823 Pius VII.
- 1808 Baltimore raised to rank of archdiocese.
- 1823–1829 Leo XII.
- 1829–1830 Pius VIII.
- 1829 First Provincial Council of Baltimore.
- 1829–1866 Irish Era.
- 1831–1846 Gregory XVI.
- 1833 Second Provincial Council of Baltimore.
- 1834 Ursuline convent burned in Charlestown, Massachusetts, signals rise of nativist agitation which continues in varying degrees for the next century.
- 1837 Third Provincial Council of Baltimore.
- 1840 Fourth Provincial Council of Baltimore.
- 1843 Fifth Provincial Council of Baltimore.
- 1846–1878 Pius IX.
- 1846 Sixth Provincial Council of Baltimore.
- 1849 Seventh Provincial Council of Baltimore.
- 1852 First Plenary Council of the United States.
- 1864 *Syllabus of Errors* issued in Rome.
- 1866–1919 German Era.

Appendix

- 1866 Second Plenary Council of the United States.
- 1870 Vatican I declares the pope infallible in matters of faith and morals.
- 1874 Questionnaire sent to American hierarchy by Vatican on the school question.
- 1875 Papal instruction issued on schools.
- 1878–1903 Leo XIII.
- 1884 Third (and last) Plenary Council of the United States issues decree making Catholic parochial schools mandatory.
- 1890–1900 Americanist controversy.
- 1903–1914 Pius X.
- 1904 National Catholic Educational Association formed.
- 1914–1922 Benedict XV.
- 1918 Revised Code of Canon Law issued in Rome.
- 1919–1958 Golden Age of American parochial school system.
- 1919 Pastoral letter of American hierarchy issued. National Catholic Welfare Conference created in Washington, D. C.
- 1922–1939 Pius XI.
- 1925 U. S. Supreme Court upheld the constitutional right to existence of parochial schools in the Oregon case.
- 1929 *Divini illius Magistri* issued in Rome.
- 1930–1945 Catholic schools temporarily decline in numbers during the depression and war years.
- 1958–1963 John XXIII.
- 1958 – – – present American Era.
- 1962–1965 Vatican II.
- 1965 Catholic schools in U. S. reach zenith in terms of enrollment and in the number of units.

TABLE I. The Catholic Parochial School System in 1900[1]

Archdiocese	Number of Parochial Schools	Number of Students	Catholic Population
Boston	61	39,000	610,000
New York	190	48,417	825,000
Cincinnati	100	26,472	190,000
Saint Louis	138	24,430	212,380
Chicago	130	48,200	700,000
Milwaukee	150	27,703	237,900
Saint Paul	79	14,230	215,000
Baltimore	81	21,077	245,000
New Orleans	106	15,721	325,000

1. From: *The Catholic Directory, Almanac and Clergy List for 1900* (Milwaukee: M. H. Wiltzius, 1900).

TABLE II. The Catholic Schools in America[1]

Year	Number of Parochial Schools	Number of Students Enrolled in Parochial Schools	Total Catholic Population in U.S.
1875	1,444		5,761,242
1876	1,645		5,620,900
1877	1,587		5,450,950
1878	2,130		
1879	1,958		6,375,630
1880	2,246	405,234	6,143,222
1881	2,389	428,383	6,367,330
1882	2,476	399,188	6,370,658
1883	2,491	428,642	6,832,954
1884	2,532	481,834	6,623,176
1885	2,464	490,581	
1886	2,621	492,949	
1887	2,697	537,725	
1888	2,606	511,063	
1889	3,024	585,965	7,855,295
1890	3,209	654,838	8,301,367
1891	3,277	665,328	8,579,966
1892	3,406	700,753	6,250,045
1893	3,587	738,269	8,806,095
1894	3,732	765,988	8,902,033
1895	3,731	775,070	9,077,865
1896	3,361	796,348	9,410,790
1897	3,438	812,611	9,596,427
1898	3,636	819,575	9,856,622
1899	3,581	815,063	9,907,412
1900	3,811	854,523	10,129,677
1901	3,812	903,980	10,774,982
1902	3,857	919,378	10,976,757
1903	3,978	963,683	11,289,710
1904	4,001	986,088	11,887,317
1905	4,235	1,031,378	12,462,793

TABLE II (Continued)

Year	Number of Parochial Schools	Number of Students Enrolled in Parochial Schools	Total Catholic Population in U.S.
1906	4,281	1,066,207	12,651,944
1907	4,364	1,096,842	13,089,353
1908	4,443	1,136,906	13,877,426
1909	4,703	1,197,913	14,235,451
1910	4,845	1,237,251	14,347,027
1911	4,972	1,270,131	14,618,761
1912	5,119	1,333,786	15,015,569
1913	5,256	1,360,761	15,154,158
1914	5,403	1,429,859	16,067,985
1915	5,488	1,456,206	16,309,310
1916	5,588	1,497,949	16,564,109
1917	5,687	1,537,644	17,022,879
1918	5,748	1,593,407	17,416,303
1919	5,788	1,633,599	17,549,324
1920	5,852	1,701,213	17,735,553
1921	6,048	1,771,418	17,885,646
1922	6,258	1,852,498	18,104,804
1923	6,406	1,922,420	18,260,763
1924	6,388	1,988,376	18,559,737
1925	6,532	2,038,624	18,654,028
1926	6,819	2,072,466	18,878,722
1927	6,995	2,167,240	19,483,296
1928	7,061	2,281,837	19,689,049
1929	7,063	2,488,682	20,112,758
1930	7,225	2,248,571	20,203,702
1931	7,387	2,283,084	20,215,098
1932	7,514	2,277,191	20,236,391
1933	7,462	2,170,102	20,268,403
1934	7,429	2,224,553	20,322,594
1935	7,442	2,209,673	20,523,053
1936	7,490	2,212,260	20,735,189

Appendix

TABLE II (Continued)

Year	Number of Parochial Schools	Number of Students Enrolled in Parochial Schools	Total Catholic Population in U.S.
1937	7,445	2,170,065	20,959,134
1938	7,428	2,101,376	21,451,460
1939	7,561	2,106,970	21,406,507
1940	7,597	2,108,892	21,403,136
1941	7,660	2,017,094	22,293,104
1942	7,701	2,065,198	22,556,242
1943	7,647	2,048,723	22,945,247
1944	7,436	1,996,209	23,419,701
1945	7,493	2,029,012	23,963,671
1946	7,493	2,070,202	24,402,124
1947	7,637	2,115,006	25,268,173
1948	7,724	2,198,212	26,075,697
1949	7,777	2,351,604	26,718,343
1950	7,914	2,477,741	27,766,141
1951	8,202	2,575,329	28,634,878
1952	8,638	2,858,171	29,407,520
1953	8,488	2,838,071	30,425,015
1954	8,493	2,992,318	31,648,424
1955	8,843	3,253,608	32,575,702
1956	9,051	3,451,785	33,574,017
1957	9,274	3,616,465	34,563,851
1958	9,653	3,828,589	36,023,977
1959	9,814	3,994,001	39,505,475
1960	9,897	4,195,781	40,871,302
1961	10,131	4,300,231	42,104,900
1962	10,177	4,370,760	42,876,665
1963	10,322	4,434,393	43,847,938
1964	10,452	4,471,415	44,874,371
1965	10,563	4,476,881	45,640,601
1966	10,550	4,409,476	46,246,175
1967	10,528	4,291,466	46,864,910
1968	10,375	4,089,926	47,468,333

TABLE II (Continued)

Year	Number of Parochial Schools	Number of Students Enrolled in Parochial Schools	Total Catholic Population in U.S.
1969	10,050	3,845,696	47,873,268
1970	9,601	3,598,096	47,872,089

1. The figures in this table are from: 1875-1889 — *Sadlier's Catholic Directory, Almanac and Ordo* (New York: D. J. Sadlier and Co., 1875-1889).

   1890-1896 — *Hoffmann's Catholic Directory and Alamanac* (Milwaukee: Hoffmann, 1890-1896).

   1898-1897 — *Hoffmann's Catholic Directory and Almanac* (Milwaukee: M. H. Wiltzius and Co., 1897, 1898).

   1899-1911 — *The Official Catholic Directory* (New York: M. H. Wiltzius, 1899-1911).

   1912-1970 — *The Official Catholic Directory* (New York: P. J. Kenedy and Sons, 1912-1970).

Suggestions For Further Reading

The best one-volume history of the American Church is Thomas T. McAvoy, *A History of the Catholic Church in the United States* (Notre Dame, 1969). John Tracy Ellis (Chicago, 1956) is, perhaps better known; and it is a short and readable account.

Monsignor Ellis has also written a good account of the early Church in *Catholics in Colonial America* (Baltimore, 1965). For the years up to the Second Plenary Council of 1866, John Gilmary Shea, *The History of the Catholic Church in the United States* (New York, 1866–1892) in four volumes is still a standard source. Henry DeCourcey, *The Catholic Church in the United States* (New York, 1856) is an obscure but, nonetheless, fascinating account, presenting an excellent index to nineteenth century thinking about the nineteenth century Church. Peter Guilday, "The Church in the United States (1870–1920): A Retrospect of Fifty Years," *Catholic Historical Review*, VI, pp. 533–547, is a brief overview of the period treated in Chapter III of this book.

The standard, general history of the Catholic parochial school system is found in the writings of Father James A. Burns: *The Growth and Development of the Catholic School System in the United States* (Chicago, 1912); *The Catholic School System in the United States: Its Principles, Origin and Establishment* (Chicago, 1908); and *The Principles, Origins and Establishment of the Catholic School System in the United States* (Chicago, 1912). His writings were later slightly revised with the assistance of Bernard J. Kohlbrenner in *A History of Catholic Education in the United States* (Chicago, 1937). The most recent history of the parochial schools is Harold A. Buetow, *Of Singular Benefit* (New York, 1970), and it is a fine elaboration and updating of the Burns-Kohlbrenner interpretation. The beginnings of revisionism can be found in Robert D. Cross, "Origins of the Catholic Parochial School System in America," *The American Benedictine Review*, XVI, No. 2 (June, 1965), pp. 194–209. Another significant study is Thomas T. McAvoy, "Public Schools vs. Catholic Schools and James McMaster," *The Review of Politics*, XXVIII, pp. 19–46.

There are many specialized studies dealing with specific aspects of American Roman Catholic educational history. The work of the Jesuits in early

America is told in Thomas Hughes, *The History of the Society of Jesus in North America, Colonial and Federal* (New York, 1907–1911). Thomas Hughes, "Educational Convoys to Europe in the Olden Time," *American Ecclesiastical Review,* XXIX, pp. 24–39, is an interesting account of some aspects of Catholic education in the colonial South. Some of the events of the stormy "Irish Era" are told in: Vincent P. Lannie, *Public Money and Parochial Education: Bishop Hughes and the New York School Controversy* (Cleveland, 1968); Vincent P. Lannie, "William Seward and Common School Education," *History of Education Quarterly,* IV, pp. 181–192; John W. Pratt, "Religious Conflict in the Development of the New York Public School System," *History of Education Quarterly,* II, pp. 140–151; and Vincent P. Lannie and Bernard C. Diethorn, "For the Honor and Glory of God: The Philadelphia Bible Riots of 1840," *History of Education Quarterly,* VIII, pp. 44–106. Lloyd P. Jorgenson analyzes the interrelationships between the private and public school movements in "The Birth of A Tradition: Historical Origins of Non-Sectarian Public Schools," *Phi Delta Kappan,* XLV, pp. 407–414. The difficulties in nineteenth century Philadelphia over Bible reading in the schools is treated in Joseph Kirlin, *Catholicity in Philadelphia* (Philadelphia, 1909). The best study on trusteeism remains Francis Tourscher, *The Hogan Schism* (Philadelphia, 1930). For insights into developments during the "German Era," Thomas T. McAvoy, *The Americanist Heresy in Roman Catholicism, 1895–1900* (Notre Dame, 1963) and Daniel F. Reilly, *The School Controversy (1891–1893)* (Washington, D. C., 1943) are invaluable. Several of the important documents of the period are reproduced in the Appendix of the Reilly study. The best explanation of the laws of the Church regarding education is Conrad H. Boffa, *Canonical Provisions for Catholic Schools* (Washington, D. C., 1939). The effects of immigration on education are taken up in: Colman J. Barry, *The Catholic Church and German Americans* (Washington, D. C., 1953); Ray A. Billington, *The Protestant Crusade, 1800–1860* (Chicago, 1964); John Higham, *Strangers in the Land: Patterns of American Nativism, 1860–1925* (New York, 1969); and Gerald Shaughnessy, *Has the Immigrant Kept the Faith? A Study of Immigration and Catholic Growth in the United States, 1790–1920* (New York, 1925). The appendices of the Barry Study contain many of the significant documents of the "German Era." Though concerned chiefly with higher education Philip Gleason, "American Catholic Higher Education: A Historical Perspective," in Robert Hassenger (ed.) *The Shape of Catholic Higher Education* (Chicago, 1967), pp. 15–53, offers many insights into the parochial school movement.

The official documents are collected in a few convenient sources. *Education: Papal Teachings* (Boston, 1960) is an indispensable index to the official writings of the popes. The periodical *The Pope Speaks* can be used to update this volume for the years after 1954. For some of the more significant encyclicals see Etienne Gilson (ed.), *The Chuch Speaks to the Modern World: The Social Teachings of Leo XIII* (Garden City, 1954) and also *Seven Great Encyclicals* (Glen Rock, 1963). William J. McGucken, *The Catholic Way in Education* (Milwaukee, 1934) is an excellent explanation of typical Catholic thinking on education up to the nineteen-sixties, and it draws heavily upon papal writings. Walter M. Abbott (ed.), *The Documents of Vatican II* (New York, 1966) is the best source for the pronouncements of the recent ecumenical council. Xavier Rynne (pseud.), *Letters from Vatican City* (New York, 1963), *The Second Session* (New York, 1964), *The Third Session* (New York, 1965), and *The Fourth Session* (New York, 1966) are an excellent supplement to Abbott. Herbert Vorgrimler (ed.), *Commentary on the Documents of Vatican II* (West Germany, 1969), in four volumes is also indispensable. John Tracy Ellis (ed.) *Documents of American Catholic History* (Milwaukee, 1962) is a good, though selected, sourcebook. Neil McCluskey (ed.), *Catholic Education in America: A Documentary History* (New York, 1964) is a useful but far from complete anthology. For the official writings of the American hierarchy through World War I, the standard source is Peter Guilday (ed.), *The National Pastorals of the American Hierarchy (1792–1919)* (Washington, D. C., 1923) with a useful supplement in Peter Guilday, *A History of the Councils of Baltimore (1791–1884)* (New York, 1932). Raphael Huber, *Our Bishops Speak, 1919–1951* (Milwaukee, 1952) includes many of the important, official writings of the bishops and of the NCWC issued after World War I. The sermons delivered at Baltimore III in 1884 are contained in *The Memorial Volume: A History of the Third Plenary Council of Baltimore, November 9 - December 7, 1884* (Baltimore, 1885). Though the decrees of this Council have not been translated from Latin, the minutes of the discussions on education have been translated and published in Francis P. Cassidy, "Catholic Education in the Third Plenary Council of Baltimore," *Catholic Historical Review*, XXXIV, pp. 257–305 and 414–436.

There were many colorful personalities in the history of the Catholic schools. Fortunately, many have already found good biographers. Peter Guilday, *The Life and Times of John Carroll* (New York, 1922) and Annabelle M. Melville, *John Carroll of Baltimore: Founder of the American Catholic Hierarchy* (New York, 1955) are standard sources on the life of the first bishop. Hugh J. Nolan, *The Most Reverend Francis Patrick Kenrick, Third Bishop of Philadelphia 1830–1851* (Washington, D. C., 1948) treats of the bishop who was confronted by the Philadelphia Bible riots. Though very dated, John R. Hassard, *Life of the Most Reverend John Hughes, D.D.* (New York, 1866) is still an interesting treatment of the Irishman who battled the nativists in mid-nineteenth century New York. Robert I. Gannon, *The Cardinal Spellman Story* (London, 1963) is also an interesting but far from objective study of the battling Irishman of the twentieth century. John Tracy Ellis, *John Lancaster Spalding: First Bishop of Peoria, American Educator* (Milwaukee, 1961) is a published version of a Gabriel Richard Lecture Series and provides some fine insights into the great nineteenth century champion of higher education who was so instrumental in the founding of Catholic University. Monsignor Ellis has also written the standard biography of Archbishop Gibbons in *The Life of James Cardinal Gibbons, Archbishop of Baltimore, 1834–1921* (Milwaukee, 1952). Frederick J. Zweirlein's *The Life and Letters of Bishop McQuaid* (Rochester, 1927), in three volumes, is perhaps best described as monumental and provides an invaluable guide to the conservative position on the school controversy of the late nineteenth century.

There is a vast amount of literature on some of the more current issues in Catholic education. Paul Blanshard's *Religion and the Schools: The Great Controversy* (Boston, 1963) is interesting but the author's notorious anti-Catholic biases make it difficult to take this book terribly seriously. Sister

Mary Janet, *Catholic Secondary Education: A National Survey* (Washington, D. C., 1949) presents an overview of the schools in the halcyon days before Vatican II. Some of the more significant offerings in the spate of "socological" studies of the schools would include Joseph H. Fichter, *Parochial School: A Sociological Study* (Notre Dame, 1958); Andrew M. Greeley and Peter H. Rossi, *The Education of American Catholics* (Garden City, 1966); and Reginald A. Neuwein (ed.), *Catholic Schools in Action: The Notre Dame Study of Catholic Schools in the United States* (Notre Dame, 1966). Mary Perkins Ryan's *Are Parochial Schools the Answer? Catholic Education in the Light of the Council* (Chicago, 1964) generated much discussion as well as Roy J. Deferrari's *Complete System of Catholic Education Is Necessary: A Reply to "Are Parochial Schools the Answer?"* (Boston, 1964). George N. Shuster presents some rather sensible observations in *Catholic Education in a Changing World* (Chicago, 1967). Another book that, unfortunately, has often been overlooked is Edward Wakin and Joseph Scheuer, *The De-Romanization of the American Catholic Church* (New York, 1966). Edmond G. Drouin, *The School Question: A Bibliography on Church-State Relationships in American Education 1940–1960* (Washington, D. C., 1963) is an invaluable reference tool for the period.

Certainly more and not less literature will be written on Catholic education in the years to come as the debates over the value of parochial education and over public aid wax.

Index

Americanist Controversy, 65-66, 67
Anglican Church. See Episcopal Church.
Are Parochial Schools the Answer? (1964), 111
Atlanta Compromise (1895), 36
Awful Disclosures of Maria Monk, 21

Baltimore Councils. See Councils of the Roman Catholic Church.
Barnard, Henry, 13, 22
Barry, John, 9
Bayley, James Roosevelt, 13, 48
Bedini, Gaetano, 34-35
Benedict XV, Pope, 69, 73-74, 82, 83, 95, 108
Bennet Law Controversy, 60-61
Bienville, Sieur de, 3
Blaine, James, 44
Bocquillon, Thomas, 60
Bohemia Manor, 7-8, 11
Brownson, Orestes, 116
Burns, James, 16, 31

Carroll, John, 7, 8, 11-13, 15, 24, 59, 91, 110
Catechism, defined, 18n4
Catholic "Conant Reports", 94
Catholic University, 35
Charlestown Convent Burning, 21, 30
Chatard, Francis, 54

Christian Education of Youth. See *Divini illius Magistri*.
Cincinnati, Archdiocese of, 48-50, 58, 68, 78n17
Cincinnati, Second Provincial Council of (1858), 58
Clement XIV, Pope, 10
Cochran Case (1930), 89-90
Codex of Canon Law, 74, 75, 82
Conant, James, 98n12
Conwell, Henry, 26
Corrigan, Michael, 56, 60, 72
Councils of the Roman Catholic Church
  Defined, 19n12
  Ecumenical: Trent (16th century), 8-9; Vatican I (1870), 69; Vatican II (1962-1965), 29, 101, 102-109, 111, 116
  Provincial: Baltimore, First (1829), 15-17, 20, 37; Baltimore, Second (1833), 28-29; Baltimore, Third (1837), 29; Baltimore, Fourth (1840), 29-31; Baltimore, Fifth (1843), 32; Baltimore, Sixth (1846), 32; Baltimore, Seventh (1849), 32; Cincinnati, Second (1858), 58
  Plenary of the United States (Baltimore): First (1852), 32-34; Second (1866), 35-37, 48, 50, 58;

137

Third (1884), 49, 52-59, 60, 65, 68, 70, 71-72, 75, 80, 108, 113
Council of Vaison (529), 8
Cross, Robert, quoted 77n14, quoted 78, 79n24

Dana, Richard, 44, 76n1
Declaration on Christian Education (1965), 29, 102-109
Decree of the Bishops' Pastoral Office in the Church (1965), 106-107
Decree on the Appropriate Renewal of Religious Life (1965), 107
Decrees on Education: 1829 (First Provincial Council of Baltimore), 15; 1852 (First Plenary Council of the United States), 33; 1858 (Second Provincial Council of Cincinnati), 58; 1866 (Second Plenary Council of the United States), 35; 1884 (Third Plenary Council of the United States), 54-55
DePauw, Edmund, 48
Diu Satis (1800), 14
Divini illius Magistri (1929), 29, 42n10, 42n11, 83-87, 88, 90, 95, 97, 99, 104, 108, 114
Documents of the American Hierarchy on Education, 40, 88-91, 114-115, 123-124
  Pastoral Letters: 1829, 15-16; 1833, 28-29; 1837, 29; 1840, 29-31; 1843, 32; 1844, 32; 1852, 33-34, 38; 1866, 35-36; 1884, 56-57; 1919, 81-82
Documents of the Popes on Education, 10, 11, 14, 27, 29, 37-40, 41, 42n11, 48, 49, 50-52, 59, 65-66, 69-76, 77n6, 77n11, 82, 83-87, 88, 90, 95-97, 99-102, 104, 105, 108, 114, 123-124
Dominus ac Redemptor (1773), 10
Dongan, Thomas, 7

Ecumenical Councils. *See* Councils of the Roman Catholic Church.
Edes, Ella B., 48, 59-60, 77n11
Education and the Redeemed Man. See Divini illius Magistri.
Elementary and Secondary Education Act (1965), 90
Emmitsburg Free School, 13
England, John, 15, 29-30, 31
Episcopal Church, 6, 7, 11, 12, 25
Ex Hac Apostolicae (1789), 11

Faribault (Stillwater) Controversy, 62-64
Feehan, Patrick, 53
Fitzgerald, Edward, 53-54, 77n13
Franciscans, 2-3
Franklin, Benjamin, 11
Freeman's Journal, 48
Froebel, Frederick, 59
Fribourg Letter (1864), 48, 77n6

Georgetown, 10, 12, 14
Gibbons, James, 52, 59, 60, 61, 72, 81
Grant, Ulysses, 44
Greeley, Andrew, 112-113
Gregory XVI, Pope, 37
Guilday, Peter, quoted 12-13, 16

Hawley, Gideon, 32
Herman's Manor, 7. *See also* Bohemia Manor.
Hochwalt, Frederick, 69, 89
Hughes, John, 7, 23, 24, 26, 28, 29, 59, 89, 92

Imprimatur, defined, 82-83
Instruction of 1875, 50-52, 59, 75, 77n11
Ireland, John, 58-59, 60-62, 63, 98n6

James II (King of England), 6, 7
Jesuits (Society of Jesus), 5, 10, 11, 14, 37, 55
John XXIII, Pope, 96, 98-102, 108, 116
Johnson, George, 69

Keane, John, 58-59
Kennedy, John F., 80, 101
Kenrick, Francis, 23-24, 26, 32-33
Kenrick, Peter, 24, 33
Know-Nothingism, 28
Koob, C. Albert, 69

Leo XII, Pope, 14, 37
Leo XIII, Pope, 39, 54, 61, 63-64, 65, 69-73, 74, 86, 98n6
Lutheran Schools, 25, 31, 46

Index

McAvoy, Thomas, 26, quoted 77n11
McCollum Case (1948), 63
McGucken, William, quoted 85, 86, 88
McMaster, James, 48-51, 54, 59-60, 76n5, 77n11
McMaster Memorial (1874), 48-50
McQuaid, Bernard, 59-60, 61, 64-65, 72, quoted 113
Madison, James (Bishop), 11, 12
Mann, Horace, 13, 14, 22, 42, 43n15
Marechal, Ambrose, 13-14, 15, 17
Monk, Maria, 21, 111
Montessori, Maria, 102
Mussolini, Benito, iii

National Catholic Education Association, 69
National Catholic Welfare Conference, 88, 89, 95, 114
National Committee of Bishops, 114
Neale, Leonard, 8, 13, 15
Newman, John, 70
Nihil obstat, defined, 82

O'Connell, Daniel, 20
Oregon Case (1925), 45, 84

Pace, Edward, 81
Pacem in Terris (1963), 100
Papal Writings. *See* Documents of the Popes on Education. *See also* Specific Titles.
Pascendi Dominici Gregis (1907), 73
Pastoral Constitution of the Church in the Modern World (1965), 105
Pastoral Letters. *See* Documents of the American Hierarchy on Education.
Paul VI, Pope, 101-103, 108
Pius VI, Pope, 11
Pius VII, Pope, iii, 14, 27, 29, 37, 83
Pius VIII, Pope, 37
Pius IX, Pope, 32, 34, 37, 38-39, 49, 69-70, 74
Pius X, Pope, 66, 69, 73, 74, 82
Pius XI, Pope, 29, 42n10, 62-63, 83-87, 88, 91, 95, 97, 102, 104, 105, 106, 108, 114
Pius XII, Pope, 95-96, 99, 100, 102, 108
Plenary Councils. *See* Councils of the Roman Catholic Church.
Propaganda de Fide, 11, 14, 18n6, 38, 50
Provincial Councils. *See* Councils of the Roman Catholic Church.
Purcell, John, 48

Quadragesimo Anno (1931), 105

Released Time, 62-63, 90
Rerum Novarum (1891), 39, 71
Roosevelt, Eleanor, 91-92
Rossi, Peter, 112-113
Rossiter Clinton, quoted 5-6
Ryan, Mary Perkins, 111-112

Saint Mary's School, Philadelphia, 8-9, 25, 26
Satolli, Francis, 64-65
Seabury, Samuel, 11
Sertum Laetitiae (1939), 95
Seton, Elizabeth Bayley, 13
Seward, William, 22-23, 28, 44
Shared Time, 62-63
Sheen, Fulton, 60
Smith, Alfred E., 80
Sollicitudo omnium ecclesiarum (1814), 14
Spalding, John, 53, 58-59, 60, 62, 64
Spalding, Martin, 35
Spellman, Francis, 91-93, 104
Stillwater (Faribault) Controversy, 62-64
Subsidiarity, Principle of, 104-105
Syllabus of Errors (1864), 39-40, 49, 70
Syllabus on Modernism (1907), 66, 82, 88

Testem Benevolentiae (1899), 62, 65-66
Tolerari: Potest (1893), 62
Trustee Controversy, 15, 21, 25-27, 29

Ursulines, 3, 21

Vaison, Council of (529), 8
Visitation Academy, 10

Washington, Booker T., 36
Washington, George, 12
Whitfield, James, 15

Zorach Case (1952), 62